Exmoor Tales
Spring

Exmoor Tales
Spring

Edited by Sarah Dawes

Layout and cover design by Oliver Tooley

Interior font - Garamond 14pt

Title font Black Chancery and Baskerville Old Face

Published by Blue Poppy Publishing, Devon

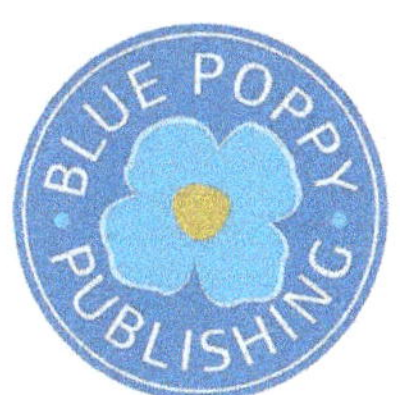

ISBN: 978-1-83778-003-7

For Ollie, Lexie and Zack
The brightest stars in the night sky.

Contents

All Quiet on the Western Front

I've had my seven-month-old grandson to stay with me this week. Now, after seven days of hilarity, hoots of laughter, and tears, the cottage walls are settling back into place. The solid bricks finding their place in the foundations that hold the cottage strong. It's all quiet on the Western Front.

I wouldn't swap the time that I spend with my grandson – to gaze deeply into his stunningly bright and smiling blue eyes reduces me to tears. To see into the very soul of his being conjures up a bond so powerful that it will remain for life and beyond. Two hearts – that of a nana and her grandchild. A very simple pleasure.

I miss him, now that he has returned home, but the cottage has regained its equilibrium of peace and calm after being 'Baby Central' for a week. It's bittersweet, this peacefulness. I'm torn between two pleasures: that of being alone, free to do as I please, when I please, and that of being in the company of my grandson, passing on knowledge (as young as he is) and rejoicing in his being with me, here on Exmoor. I know I'm allowed a mixture of both and that suits me fine. I suppose it's the light and shade of life and we need both to survive, to make life interesting.

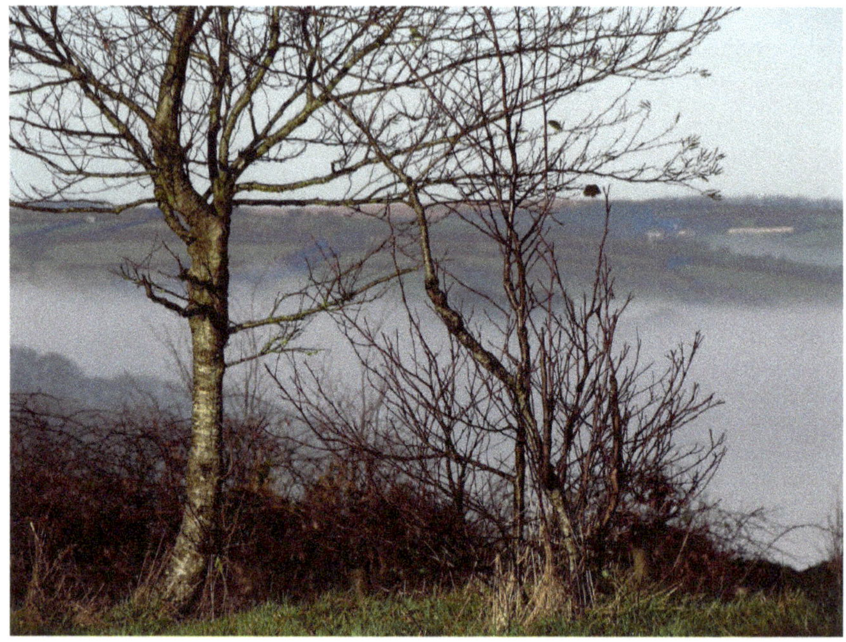

Waving them off down the lane, early on Sunday morning, I stood there in my fleecy pyjamas, which were tucked down into my Dublin boots to prevent them becoming soggy. The day had dawned wet and breezy and there was a white mist hovering above the road, shifting as the slight wind took it on its way across the fields. There and then I decided to take myself off across the moor to Fyldon Common, Kingsford Gate, and Simonsbath, to see what treasures I could find on this dismal day. Packed up, camera at the ready, and with my charity shop Bear Grylls fleece keeping some of the drizzly rain at bay, I was good to go, and go I did.

Mist on Exmoor is intermittent – pea soup in places and then, magically, gone. This morning was no different and I travelled down the lanes and across the moor, driving in and out of the blanket and lace-curtain swirls. On reaching my destination it was abundantly clear that there were to be no sightings of anything that morning. I was high up on the moor with, usually, excellent views to the left of me – but not today. There was just the rousing call of a pheasant coming eerily out of the dense mist.

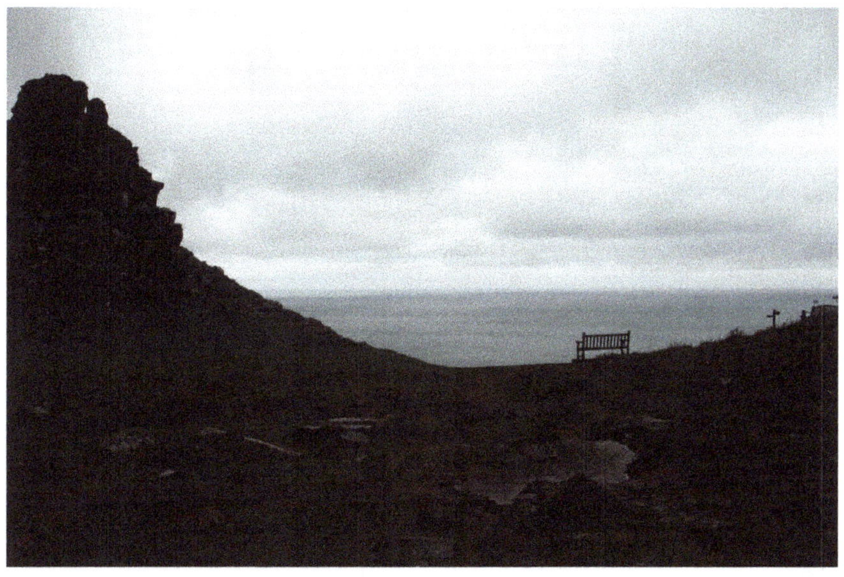

Executive decision time found me making my way towards Lynton and Lynmouth on the North Devon coast. The Valley of Rocks was somewhere I hadn't been for some years. I thought it would be a welcome change to go shout at the sea and throw my troubles into the wind on this dramatic coastline.

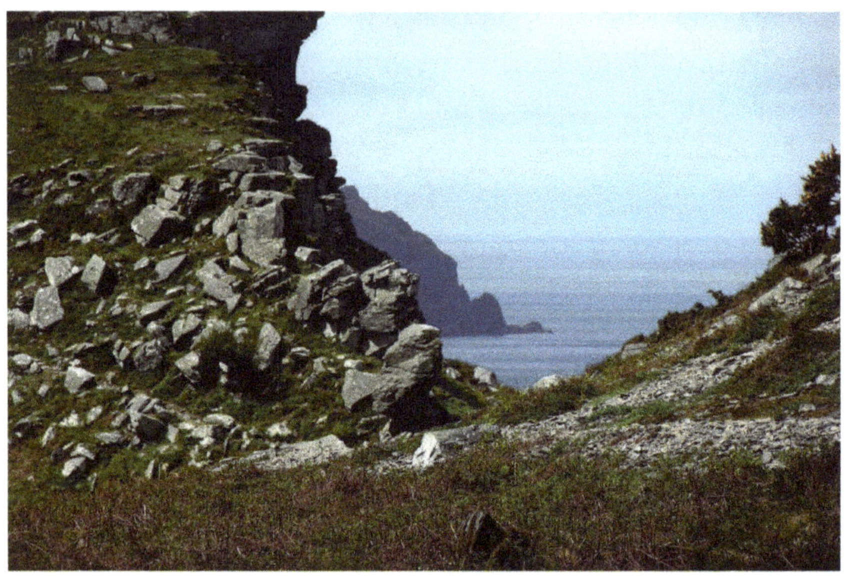

I made my way carefully through the mists and out the other side. Reaching the road to Lynton was like coming out from under a blanket after a weird dream, with all becoming clear once again, and I felt myself waking as I headed towards the brighter skies, a coffee, and a homemade cookie. The lanes there are lined with beech trees, then new with citrus green leaves that dappled the shiny road ahead of me, as the sunshine broke through them. My view changed as the undulating roads took me past lush, emerald-green fields, ancient woodlands, and sparse, wheat-coloured moorland. Here, rich fields butted up against the dry-looking moor and it made me think about our wonderfully diverse countryside.

Red deer grazed on the moor, camouflaged by their brown-grey coats but with their whitish rump giving them away. I pulled in to watch them awhile as they were quite a large herd, their heads raised at my presence but not unduly spooked by my observation.

I left them to their breakfast and followed the curving roads once again. Climbing the hills to the Valley of Rocks is quite hairy if you're not used to the roads. They are dotted with hairpin bends that come at you out of the blue, and I've been in cars where passengers have gasped out loud, clinging onto their seat, as the bends and hills are encountered, captured, and conquered!

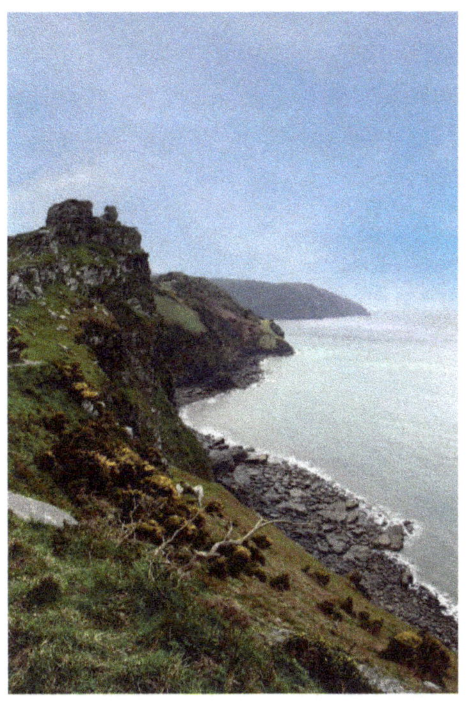

As the rocky outcrops came into sight I wondered if I'd catch a glimpse of the wild goats that roam the cliffs here but, car park in sight, my first priority was sustenance by way of a welcome coffee and something to eat. A text message from my daughter informed me that she had stopped for breakfast herself, so I thought I'd share the time with her, even though I was absent from her company.

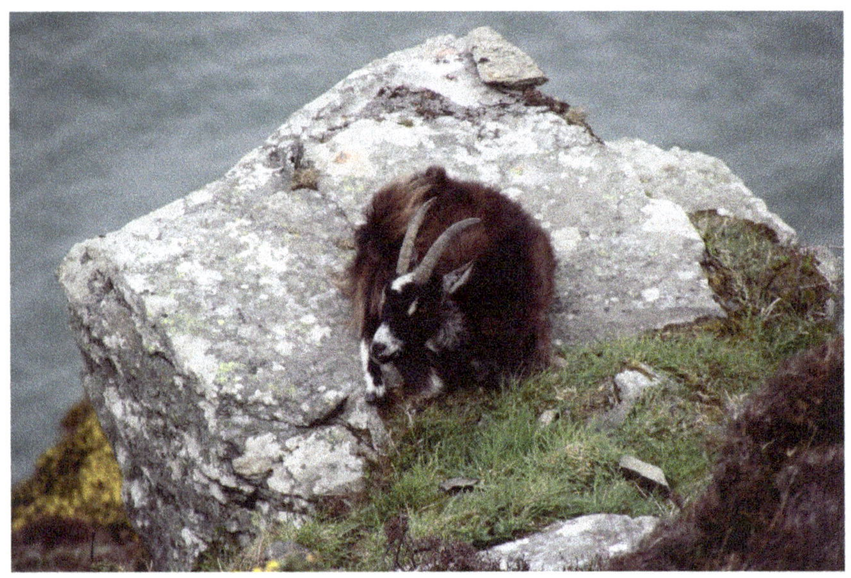

Being apart from your offspring doesn't mean they are out of mind, does it? It would give me time to ponder awhile on the week that had just passed and at how fortunate I was to have such riches in my life.

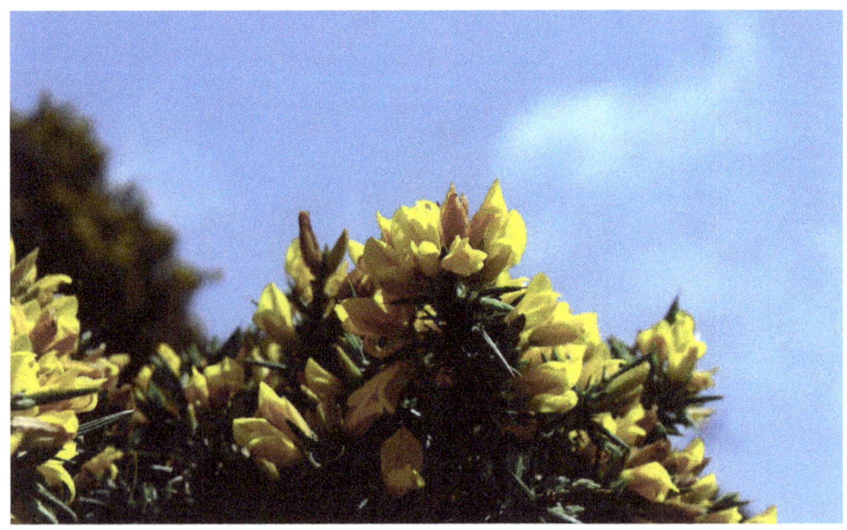

Along the Lane and Over

With a lull in the weather and a pretty clear day ahead, a wander somewhere off the beaten track seems to be the order of the day. So, with lunch and a small flask already packed up and stowed away, we set off across the fields above Dulverton.

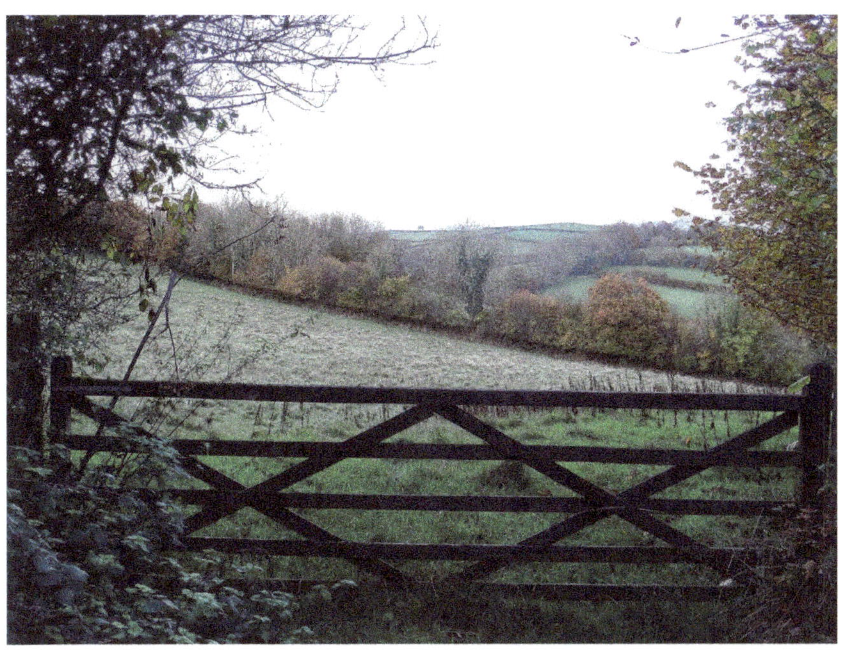

Over the years, being lucky enough to have the freedom of the surrounding fields, we've found innumerable places to rest, watch, and ponder. Today, our feet have taken us along the damp, shiny tarmac to a gateway that creaks desperately when it's opened. It's always made such a noise and it seems an intrusion into the quiet of the countryside as we close it behind us. Through the gateway and across a rutted track with beech hedgerows lining each side, we take a glance to the left and right. If we're quick, we're usually able to see around ten or so rabbits grazing close to the hedgerow. If they've hopped off before we set eyes on them, the tell-tale movement of the longer grasses lets us know they'd been there.

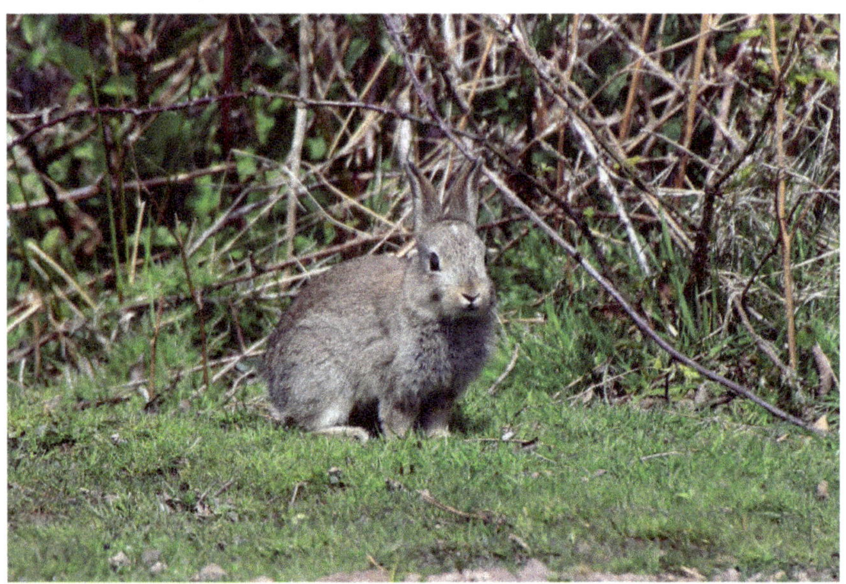

Over the muddy track we come to yet another gate. Now, this gate has been here forever; it is wooden, misshapen, and has been repaired on more than one occasion. It functions well though and does the job it is there to do, namely keeping the lambing sheep from wandering the lanes. In the summer months to come, this particular field will be full of wild flowers and grasses, being free of sheep. Swallows will dive and dart low above the growth during this time; they are amazing to watch as they make their high-pitched call to one another, but nigh-on impossible to photograph with our limited equipment; normally.

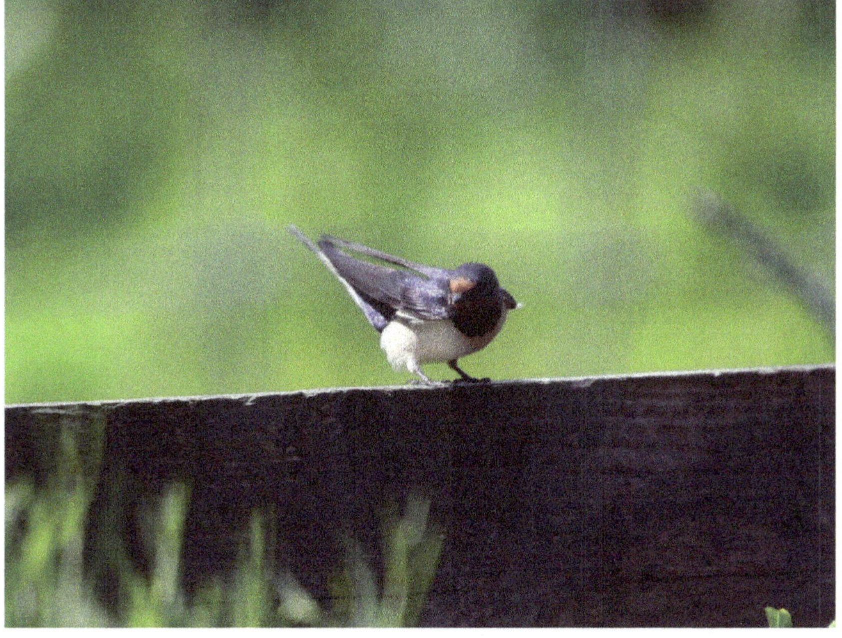

Today, though, the grass is being grazed by the ewes and their offspring. We skirt the field alongside a line of tall beech trees, accompanied by one or two rabbits, which are brave enough to venture out during the late morning hours. They scamper and hop away as we approach, waiting until their patch is no longer being trampled on by strangers before returning to nibble the sward.

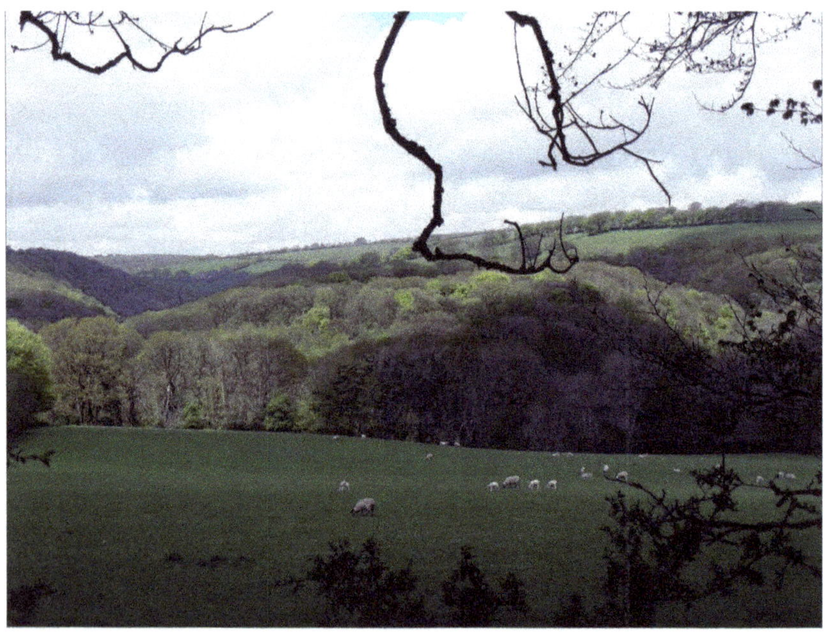

Through the beech trees to our right, there sits another field, joined to its neighbour at the top and bottom. It is a haven for bird life and we've sat for many hours in a top corner, watching the many birds as they go about their daily feeding rituals. A favourite to spot is the little olive brown chiffchaff. We can always hear it, with its unmistakable 'chiffchaff' call, but it's never quite that easy to see as it flits from branch to branch.

Today there is the continuous warbling trill of the skylark to be heard, high above us, as we wander. Skylarks will always evoke childhood memories for me, as I remember walking carefully across fields with my brother, eyes on the ground, looking to avoid the closely concealed nests with my little feet. Alternately, my head would be thrown back, gazing into a cloudless sky, trying with all my might to spot the soaring little brown bird, as it reached us with its song.

Coming to the bottom of the field, we climb a secured gate, overgrown with brambles and ivy. Deciding to take a path to the left, we walk diagonally through a scrubby, patchy field using tracks which criss-cross through thistles and tussocks of grass. The muddy, narrow tracks, made by the many wandering sheep over the years, make our crossing easy. However, today this patch of land is sheep-free and empty. We aren't harming anything by using the track and it sees us making our way downhill towards a gap in yet another line of beech trees, atop an ancient hedgerow.

This has to be one of our favourite places to stand and take in the view; for a short while we do just that. Wide-open, rolling fields and pasture land, woodland, combes, far-reaching views of farmsteads and the wildlife. We are looking towards Dulverton and a main thoroughfare in the distance, and there is always so much to look at.

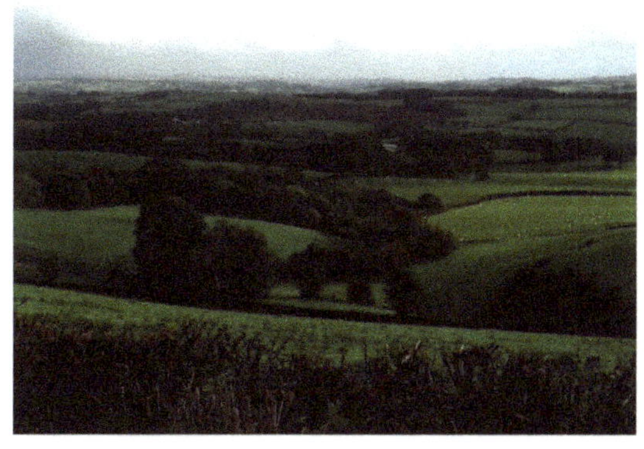

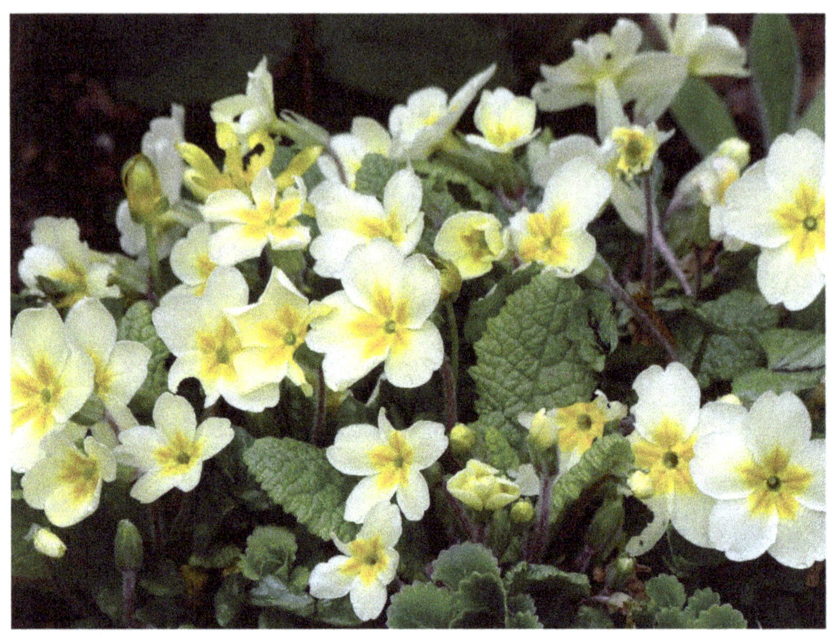

Over the years we've seen the same view change with the seasons, taking on a life of its own as it blends spring into summer, summer into autumn, autumn into winter, and winter back to spring. It's a view that we never tire of, whether we've stopped for a quick rest, leaning on a gate, or have settled down for our al fresco lunch.

To see and to feel the openness of the ever-changing countryside before you and the wide-open skies, whether blue or grey, above you, is a feeling that is so good to experience. Up here, the smallest sound is amplified and it does your soul good to sit and listen, for a short while, to the tiniest sounds of the wildlife inhabitants around you – the song of a wren, the mew of a buzzard soaring high above – but also to listen to the silence that punctuates the noises of the countryside.

Filling our lungs with Exmoor air, we wander further down, having crossed through the gap and into another lush field. At the bottom, we reach an ancient, banked hedgerow where the gnarled, twisted trees are covered with emerald-green moss. Along this bank is an extremely handy stretch, free of trees and hedging. We've really been strolling along, taking our time, and this is our lunchtime viewing point, with hot tea from the flask and our ham and mustard rolls making an appearance. As we sit, with the best view in the house stretching out as far as we can see, we chat about how we always return to the same spots – away from the lanes, and away from the usual walking routes – and how fortunate we are to be able to do so.

With an apple to see us on our way, we follow the edge of the field and walk for half a mile or so, dipping downwards on a muddy track. We have horses above us, rugged up against the weather, and curious sheep to the right. Following a small brook through yellow gorse-covered land we eventually cross the tumbling water and turn right.

In the very near distance we spy a stunning-looking fox that doesn't look that perturbed to see us. It is perched on a mossy cushion of grass, looking this way and that, but fixes his eyes on us as we approach him. Without a trace of hurry about him, he leaves his position, his magnificent brush with its white tip following on behind. Making his way down the sloping field towards cover, he is gone.

We, on the other hand, have begun a tricky traverse through a spattering of trees before reaching a gradual, sloping field. This sees us trudging upwards towards the road, boots now heavy with mud. From here, we can look back the way we have come: the undulating ground that took us to the heights for our lunch, then down and back up again for the homeward-bound journey.

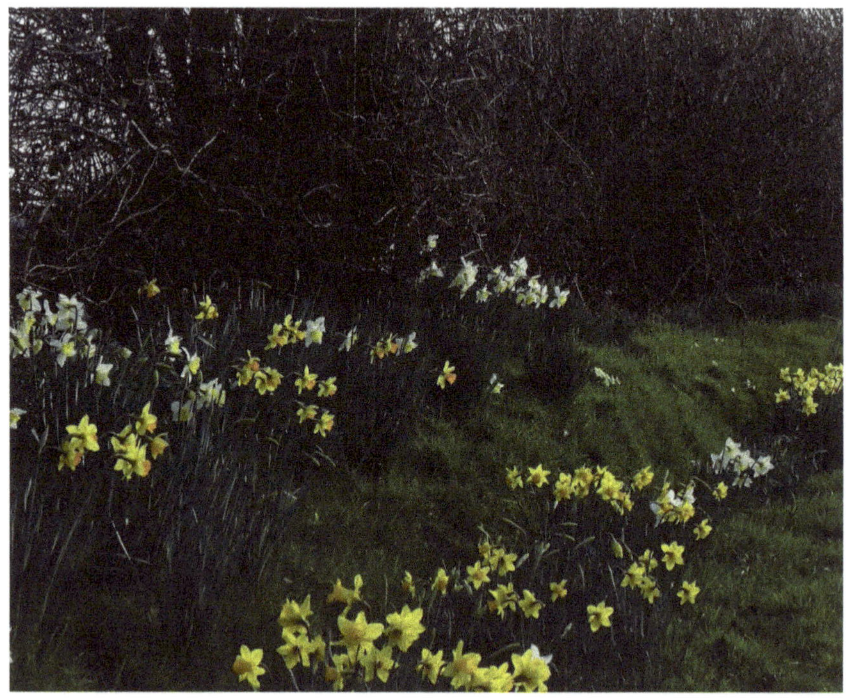

Turning left and making our way back towards the lane, we can see that spring is well on its way, as new growth is making a bid for life in the hedgerows. Daffodils, with their sunny, yellow heads, wave in the breeze, having been planted randomly, but thoughtfully, along the roadside to bring a smile to the face of anyone passing by. Spring is definitely poking its head out for all to see, and we are pleased to note that the recent snow hasn't put paid to its tentative beginnings: the flora of Exmoor is tougher than that.

After the trudge uphill, in muddy conditions, we are now on the lane. As a celebration of any of our wanders, we always treat ourselves to a stick of chocolate fudge on our return journey. So, as we make our way up the slow incline to the road home, I produce said sweets from my pocket with a flourish, giving the rambling stroll a cherry-on-top feeling.

What do I enjoy more: the walk or the celebratory stick of fudge? Hmm, no contest really – it's the walk every time – but, sometimes, you just can't have one without the other.

Dulverton: Putting the Past to Rest

Imagine, if you can, accidentally discovering, while on the internet one evening, that your dad had passed over two months previously – a dad that you'd had no contact with for nigh-on twenty years, but whom you'd always loved. This is what happened to my husband some years ago and to say he was distraught is an understatement. Apart from listening and just being there for him, I didn't know what else to do, but knew I had to do something to help him through his grief and his thoughts of all those lost years. So, with a determined effort, and his blessing, I began to carry out a little research.

My husband's dad was a very special man; he had a heart of gold and I got on exceptionally well with him, so this was something I needed to do. You see, we've always felt a pull towards Exmoor and walked the lonely moors, the rugged woodlands, and tumbling rivers whenever time was kind to us. There was an extra pull towards Dulverton for one reason only: we knew my husband's grandmother had been evacuated there from London, during the war, and also knew that's where his father had been born – in the parish of Dulverton. What we didn't know was where exactly, but the pull towards Exmoor and Dulverton was even stronger now that he was no longer with us.

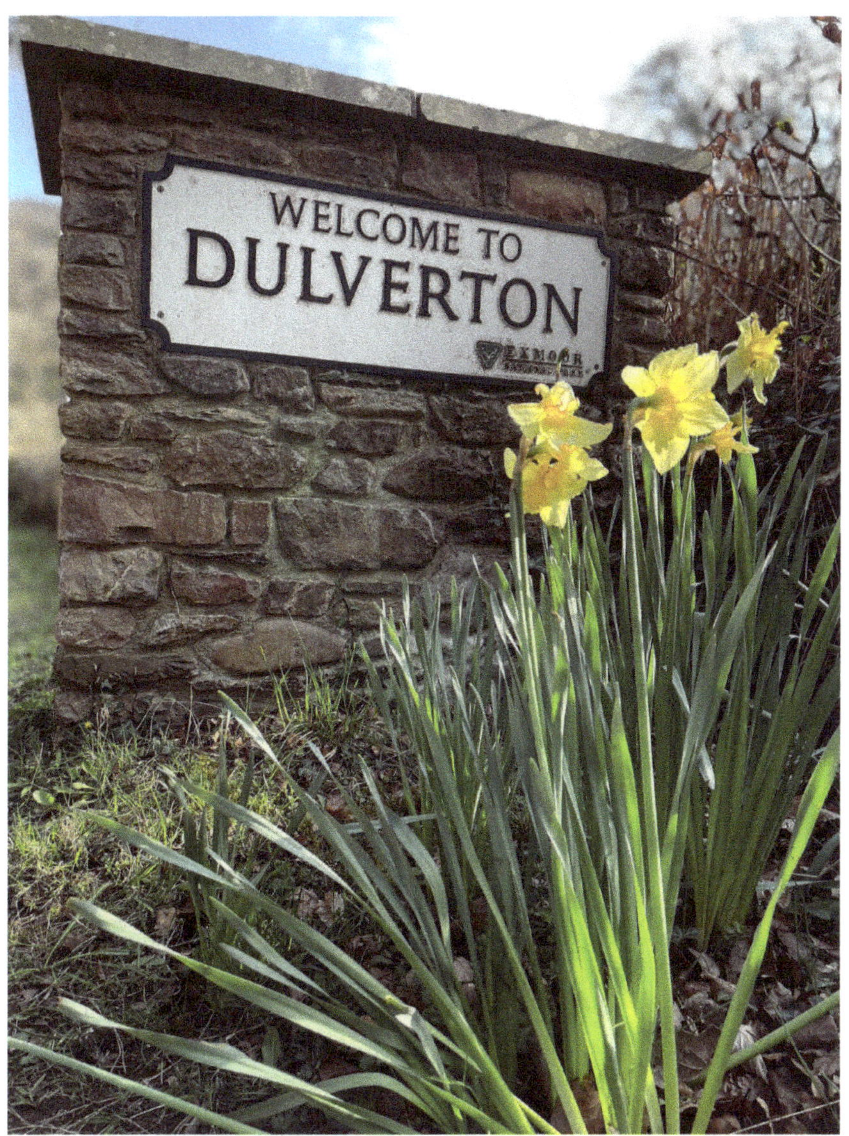

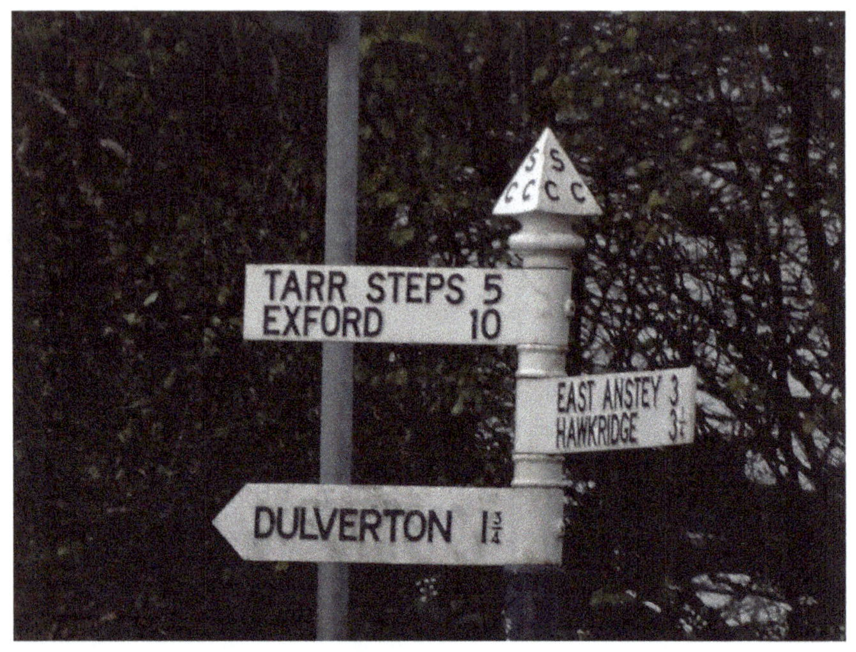

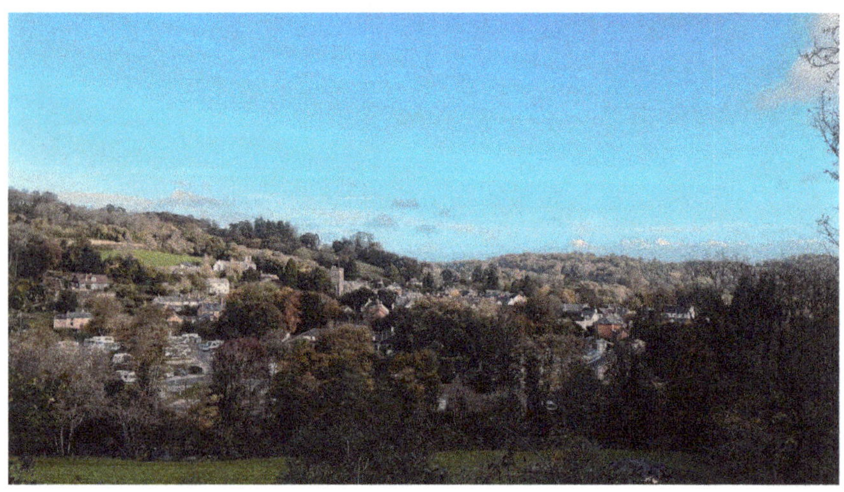

Gathering as much information as I could, and eventually purchasing his birth certificate, I found that he was born in a large, sprawling farmhouse on the edge of

Dulverton. I won't give out the name of the farm, because it still stands and is still known by the same name. I'd further learnt that his grandmother, pregnant at the time, had been housed at the farm along with several other girls. They were expected to work both in the house and on the land with the animals.

Now, at least, we knew where his father had been born. With all the information in hand, I booked us into the welcoming Exmoor Forest Inn, in Simonsbath, for a couple of nights. Not too close to Dulverton, but not too far away. It's a place we had stayed in regularly and I knew that it would do us both good to have a bit of peace and quiet.

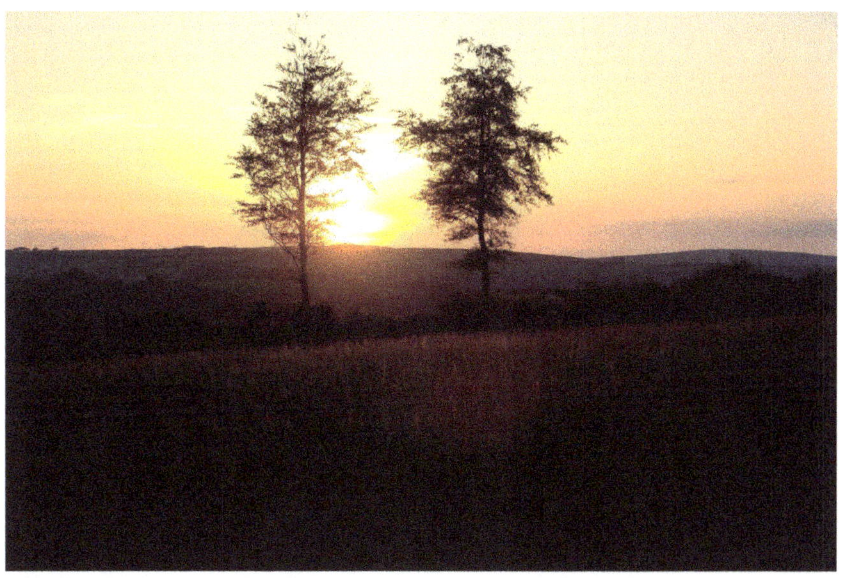

Morning came and, having had a delicious and hearty breakfast, we made our way over to Dulverton, across a misty moor, to visit All Saints' church in the vibrant, pretty town we loved so much. Having discovered where his father had been born, but not knowing if he'd been baptised or not, we decided that the church there may have been a close enough bet. We intentionally took a rather circuitous route before reaching the town, wending our way down back lanes that gave far-reaching views out over Exmoor and the Somerset countryside.

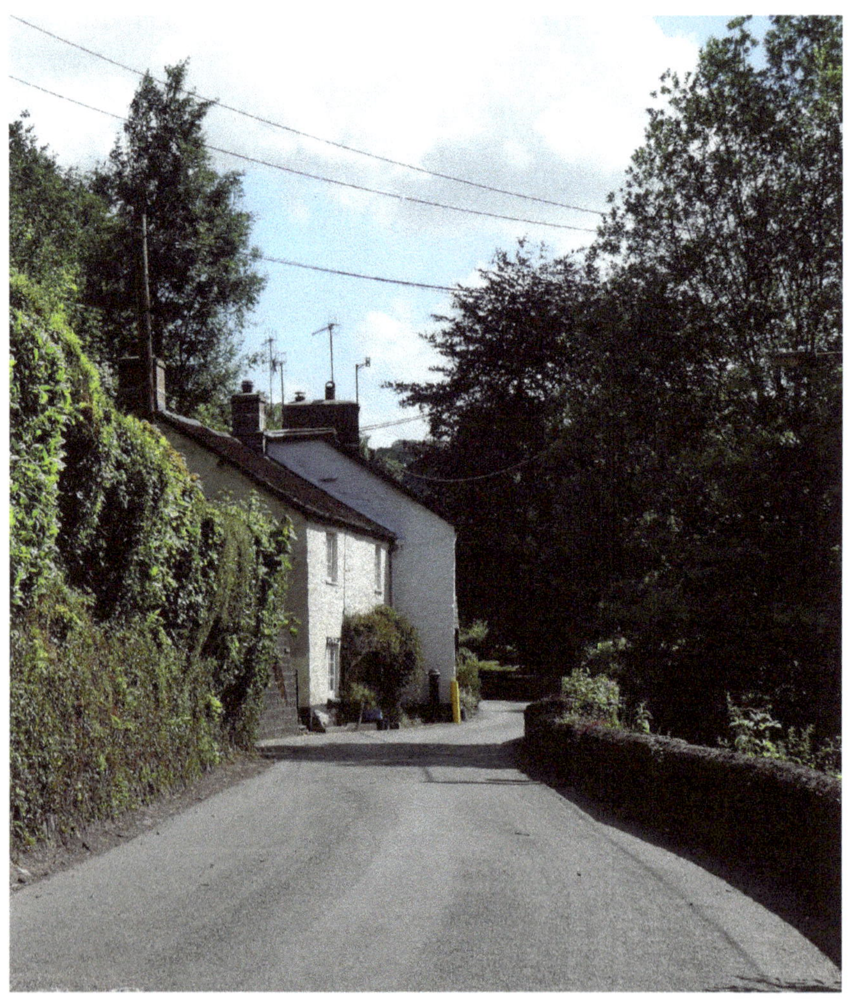

Our route took us past the farm where his dad had begun his days and we logged the location in our memories for all time. Having reached the church, what greeted us as we entered the grounds was incredible. Before us was a carpet of crocuses in purples, yellows, and white. It was stunningly beautiful and it seemed as if the sun had come out and shone down on us, despite the chill of the day. It made us smile and neither of us felt any sadness in any way.

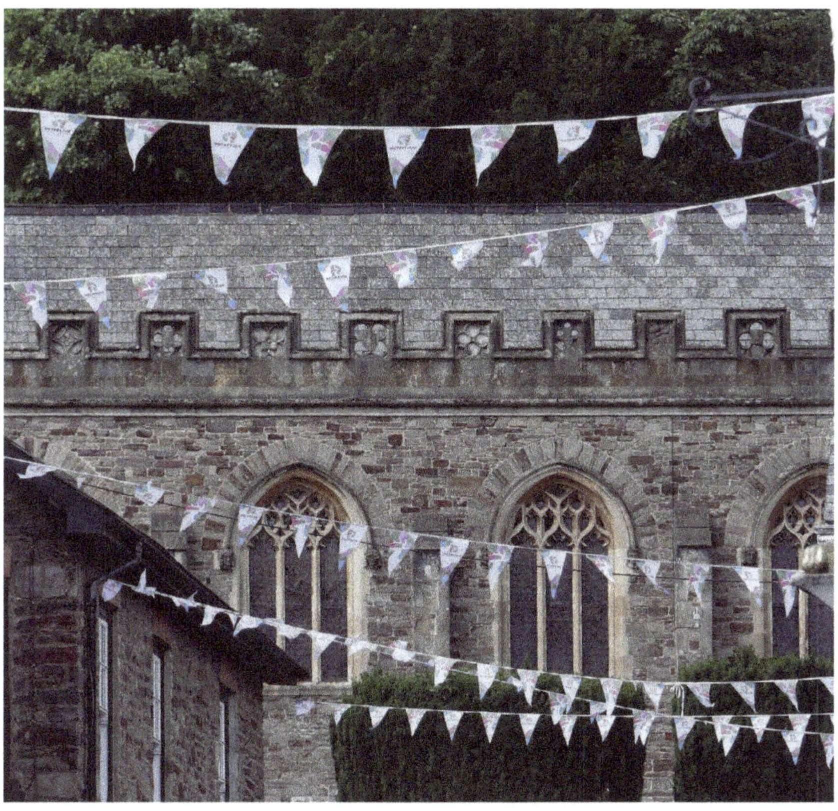

As we entered the church, we were greeted and warmly welcomed by an elderly lady with a beautiful smile. We explained why we were there and she listened intently,

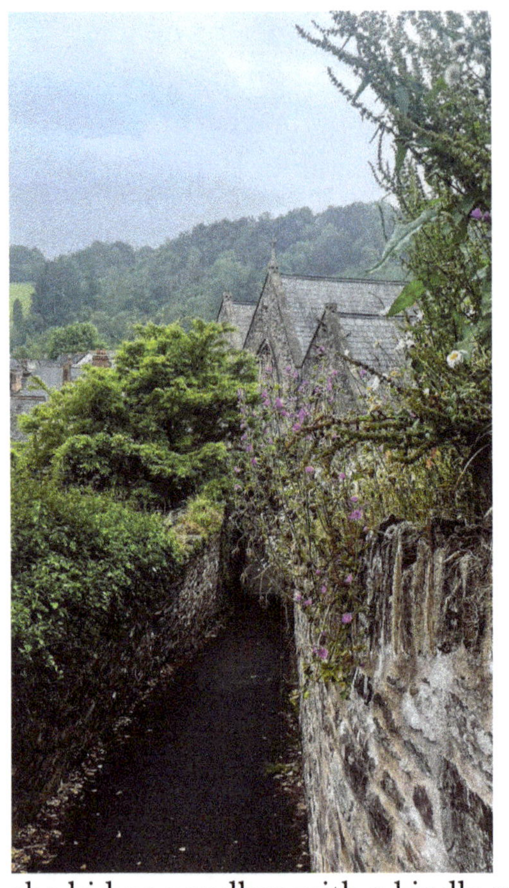

shedding extra light on the information that we already had. She was extremely helpful and knowledgeable, and offered us a candle or two to light in memory of his dad. Then she left us to ponder quietly. This we did and then sat for a while in the stillness of the church. After giving us the email address of the vicar there and telling us to visit the 'Copper Kettle' in town for a warming cup of tea, she bid us goodbye with a kindly nod of her head.

The lady thought the vicar may have been able to access parish records to see if any baptism had taken place. Sadly, the information was not forthcoming as the records had been lost, so we'll never know. But the church had fulfilled its job for us and I know that some sort of peaceful closure happened that day. Within months of that visit, we'd put our house on the market and moved from South Somerset to a cottage on the moor. The pull that we'd always felt was too strong and the decision had been made.

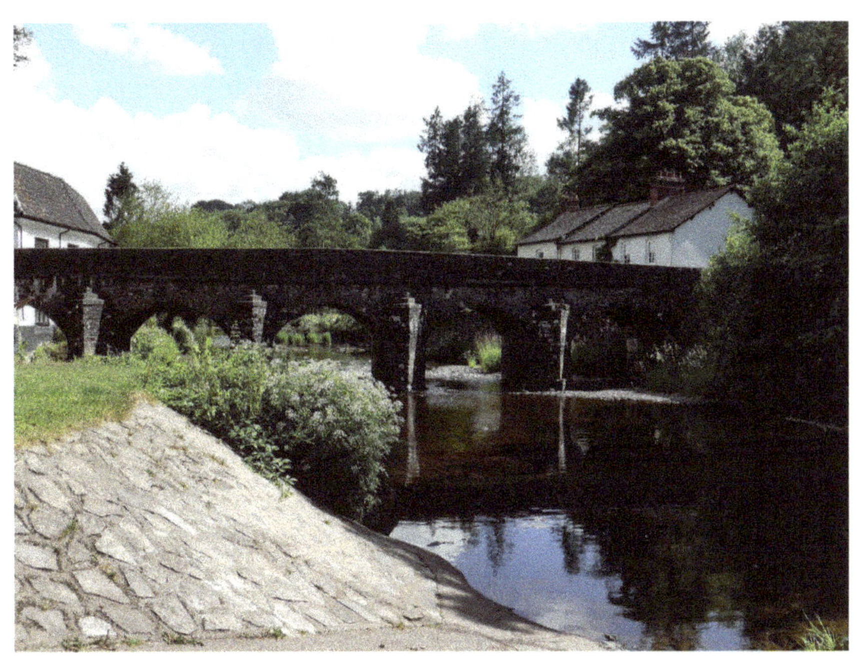

The tale doesn't end there, however. Coming along the main road to Dulverton late one afternoon, we passed a track on the left-hand side. I'm always on the lookout for wildlife – my eyes are everywhere as we travel – so it was with some interest that I spotted a russet cow making her way along the lane towards the main road. I mentioned that it didn't seem altogether right that she should be there, alone and loose.

We quickly stopped and reversed but she had beaten us to it and was out on the road, having taken a right turn, and ambling down the tarmac, udders swinging merrily. Thinking on our feet, we decided to pull across the road at an angle to prevent any further traffic passing us and causing a potential accident. Driving towards us and the cow, from the direction in which we'd come, was another car. The driver had seen us frantically waving our arms and had, thankfully, stopped and had also pulled across the road.

Now the cow was sort of boxed in, but it looked as if she was on a mission so we didn't think we had long to solve the problem. We now also had two cars at our end of the road, both stopped and both waiting patiently. They could see quite clearly what the predicament was. There was no open gateway to herd her into – it was all quite a mystery. When we explained that we would drive down the track to the farm to see if anyone was about to throw some light on the situation, one of the drivers said that he would hold the traffic. The sign for the farm was at the opening of the track and, as she'd come out of the entrance, we thought this was our best bet. So off we went, bumping down a muddy track towards the farm and outbuildings.

However, after knocking on the front and back doors and calling around the outbuildings, it was obvious there was no one at home. There was a phone number on the farm sign, which we'd taken note of. This we duly called but still no answer. The occupants were definitely out.

We returned to the road, where the cow was standing quite still in between the two blocking cars about 150 yards apart. We'd now been joined by a quad bike and trailer carrying a collie. It was being driven by a wizened elderly man, wearing a cloth cap. With his dog barking excitedly, he'd pulled over and blocked a lane on the left-hand side of the road, around midway. Between us we had the situation under control but we were still none the wiser as to who the cow belonged to. At least she was safe for the time being.

The road was blocked and any danger from vehicles was being averted. Minutes later, a red pickup and trailer appeared from down the track that we'd followed. It turned out onto the road, passing us with a thumbs-up sign. It pulled alongside and explained that the cow belonged to them but asked if we had we seen a calf with her, as they thought she'd escaped her field having gone to look for her 'lost' calf. We had to say no, we hadn't seen one. It was just the one cow, but that we'd keep an eye out for it in the adjoining fields on the journey home.

All traffic was held as the cow was loaded with no fuss and taken back to the farm. Then, everyone went their separate ways as if nothing had happened. Danger averted.

It was on the way home that we looked at each other and smiled. The reason being that we both knew we'd just been knocking on the doors of the farmhouse, where my husband's dad had been born, all those years ago, during the war. It meant the absolute world to both of us that we'd been stood there, with amazing views out towards Somerset and Devon on that late afternoon. Nobody knew our secret.

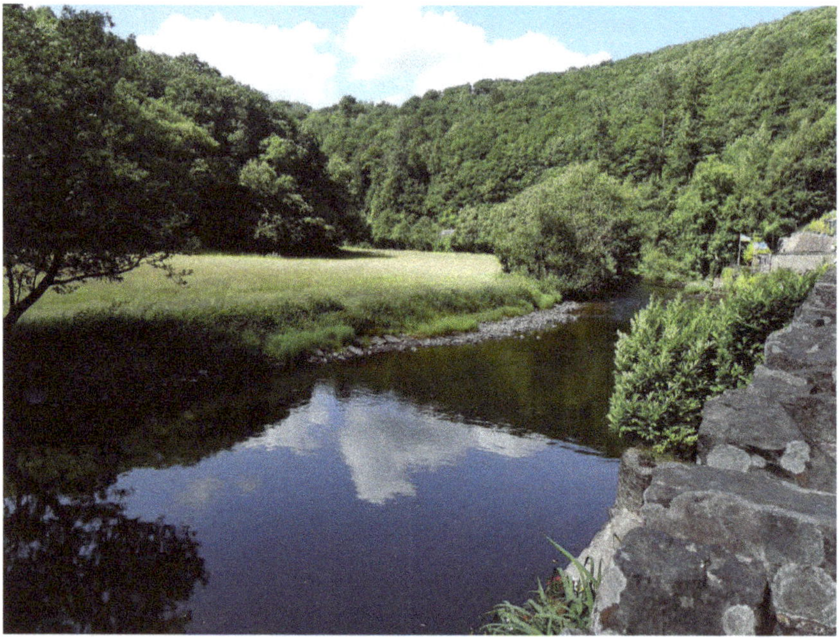

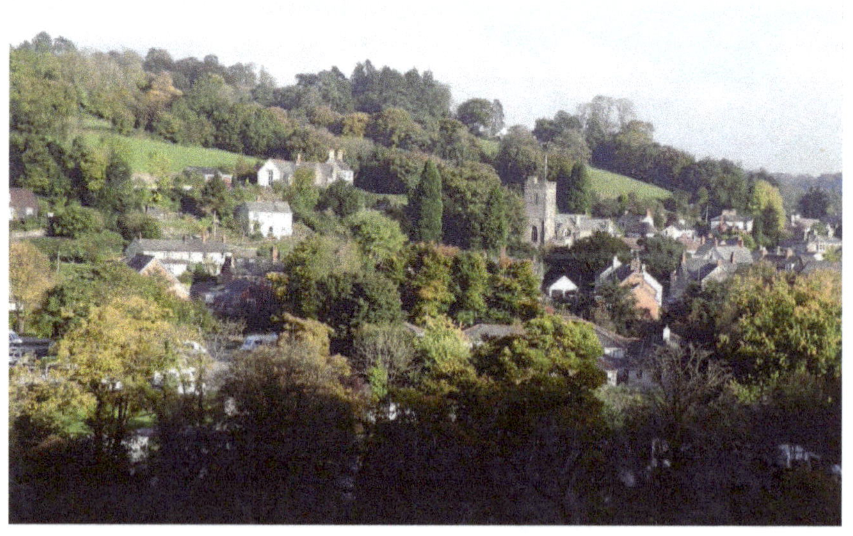

But that's not all. From our bedroom window at the front of the cottage we now lived in, we could look directly across the fields, where a herd of some eighty deer would graze in the early morning sun. Across those fields, as the crow flies, around two miles' distant and tucked down in a dip, sat the farmhouse where the dad that he loved had been born.

His birth certificate hangs on the wall in our kitchen; it has been there for years and is a constant reminder of our link with the pretty little Exmoor town. Who'd have thought it? Certainly not us. We still often wonder just who was pulling whom to Exmoor all those years ago.

Nature Is Sometimes Noisy

It's been a peculiar week for me; I've felt very adrift with the change in the weather. It's as if I've been floating about on the water without a paddle, not knowing which way to go. By now, I should be used to the change in seasons and the difference it makes to my day, but it takes a little while for me to make the transition. Due to the warm days I can dispense with clearing and laying the fire, stacking logs indoors, and collecting starters and lighters down the lane. Now my time changes to planting seeds, caring for seedlings, and working in the garden instead. There's nothing wrong with that and I love how I spend my time, but it takes a while to adjust.

This morning there was a hazy mist hovering around the fields. That was a good sign for the day to come and, sure as eggs is eggs, the sun came out and warmed the soil. The bold and beautiful magpies, their long tail feathers shining in the sun, were up and about early. One of them flew three different directions in turn, landing on the same tree each time, before returning to its nest, chattering away as only magpies can.

Colourful goldfinches, with their bright ruddy-coloured faces and yellow wing patches, are still busy in the hedge with their nest. They seem to have taken over this particular part of the hedgerow from the dunnocks, who potter about on the lawn below but keep their distance. Many think that the dunnock is a small, dull, brown bird with no character but they make my day with their velvet song, not quite matching the robin, but still as tuneful. Never a cross word does the dunnock have – they keep out of trouble and milly-mander about at the base of the bird table for most of the day.

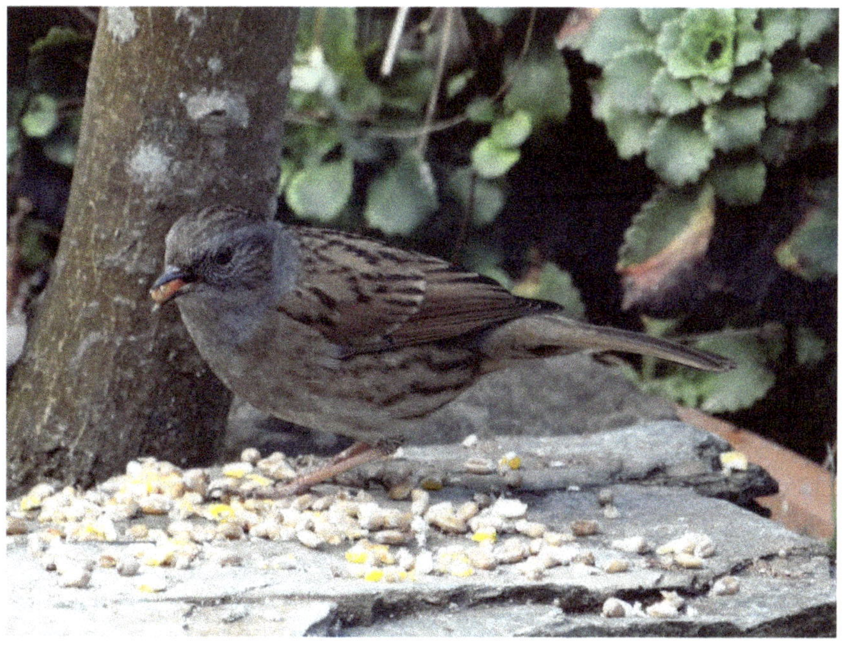

Yesterday, I had three robins at the bird table and what a scrap occurred; in all my days, I can honestly say I've never seen a robin fold itself in two before. One, puffing itself up in a show of aggression, thrust its beak in the air while its tail came to meet its beak from behind, almost completing a circle. This possessive little robin, with its very red breast, was protecting its territory with a vengeance and wasn't afraid to show off. To be fair, it does have a nest hidden low down in the hedge that runs along the back garden and, probably, a family to feed, so it has a point. The robin will routinely fly from hedge to fence post, to the corner of my raised vegetable bed, and then back again. On the way back it uses a circular route, by-passing all the posts and coming in at an angle around seven feet from the nest. When I sit at the garden table I can see this confident little bird making its way through the shrubs and branches to its destination, safely hidden away.

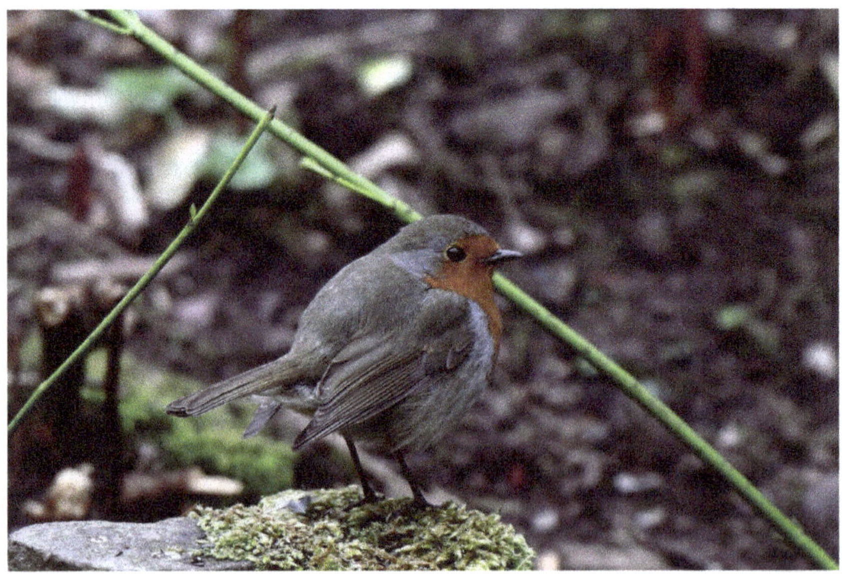

You take your life in your hands sitting at the garden table as the swallows are extremely busy too. They have nested in the eaves of the house and fly, at speed, back and forth, darting here and there on the wing, and have been known to whizz past my ears when I've been lunching in the garden. They bring a certain gaiety and joyfulness to the warm days with their constant chittering as they zoom about. Last year, when their fledglings left the nest, the parent birds fed them while they were perched on the cherry tree. It was so funny to watch as the podgy babies lined up on the branch waiting for their delivery from mum and dad. Perhaps it will be the same this year too.

~

The front windows of the cottage look over Exmoor fields and valleys and I always love to hear the sounds of the coming day as they rise into the air in the early hours. As is usual, I opened the curtains this morning and then followed with the window. A chill breeze hit my body but the noises in such a peaceful place were plentiful, and I didn't want to miss them. Goosebumps arising, I stood with my cup of tea and listened as a dog barked in the distance, together with the distinct bleating of sheep and their lambs, obviously being rounded up for one reason or another and not too happy about it.

Birdsong was the next to hit me as I stood there, still chilling – but not in the relaxed way the word sometimes means. I could pick out robins with their truly velvety song and a male blackbird with his beak so yellow it could have been dipped in a fresh egg yolk that morning. He was high on a post and calling out to the world for all his worth.

Chaffinches called with their morning refrain, one after the other, non-stop and vying for attention in the orchestra of song, and the magpies chattered away like percussion in the background. Lastly, I could hear the distant but very distinctive drone of a tractor, carrying out a daily task in the fields beyond.

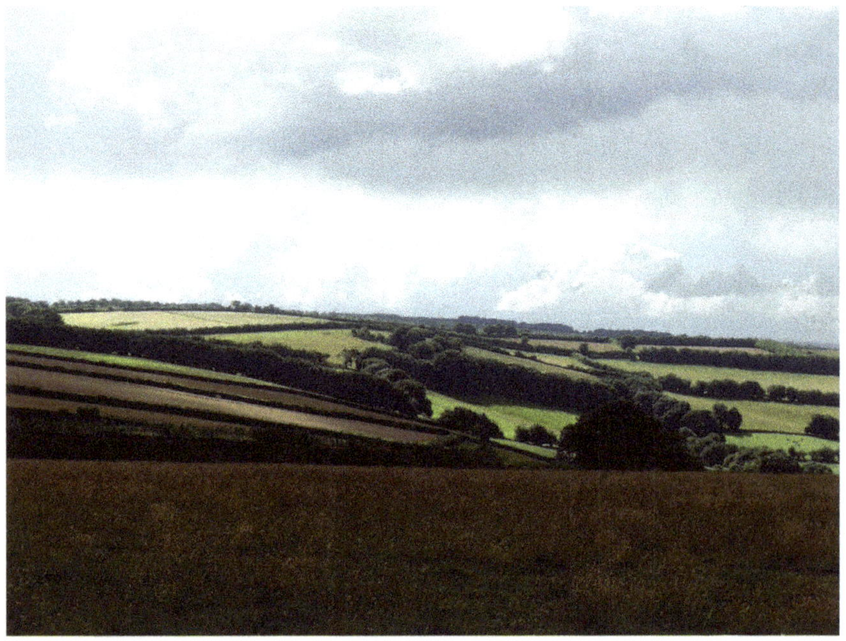

Nature can be noisy sometimes, but also very entertaining. Country sounds – you can't beat them.

Closing the window, I shivered against the chill of the air but knew it wouldn't last long. Misty morns, at this time of year, herald warm days and I was happy and content to leave the wildlife to its own devices while I readied myself for the hours in front of me.

Plans for the day involved washing the kitchen floor (necessary), replacing the elastic in a fitted sheet (it only lasts so long when it's washed so often), and baking a lemon drizzle cake – because afternoon tea without cake is just not cricket. Once I'd completed these chores (although I don't consider them chores as such), I'd be free to wander the garden and examine my herbs and plants.

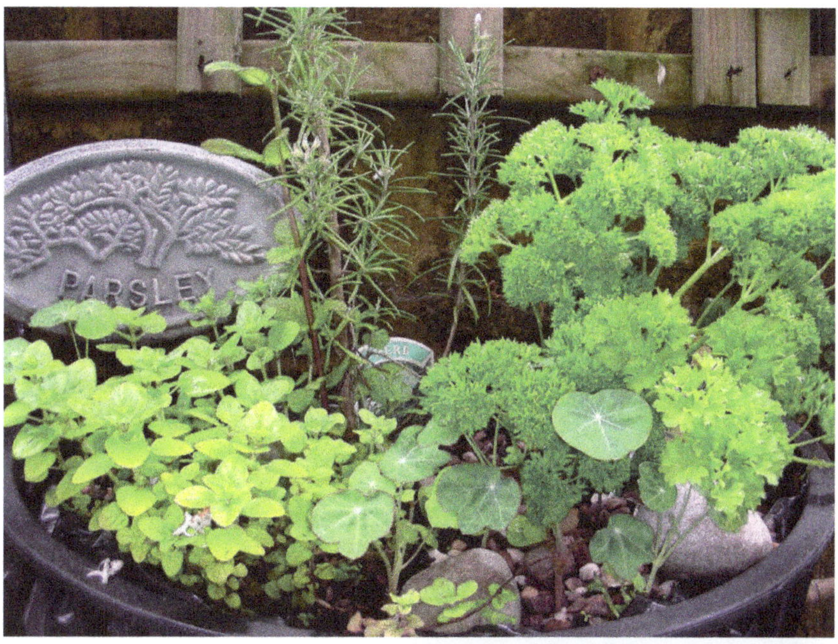

I have so many herbs that need splitting, potting up and moving: marjoram, mint, lemon balm, sage, thyme, horseradish, to name a few. I don't know where to begin but I enjoy

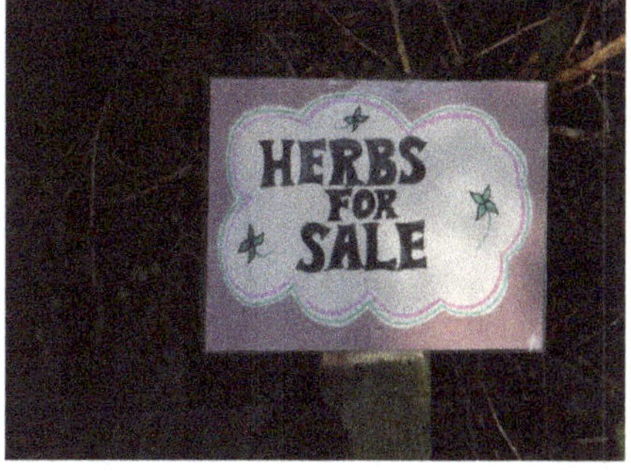

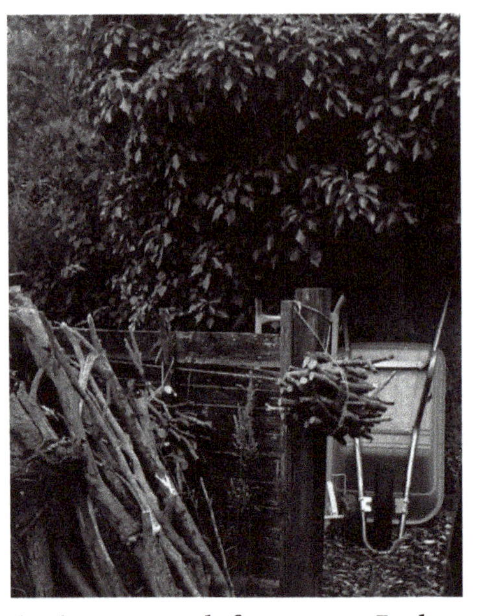

jobs such as this; it's therapy and gives me time to think on things, so I can't wait to get stuck in.

Over the previous weekend, while working in the garden, I had noticed a hen pheasant creeping down low and making her way across the field to my raised bed area. I absently asked her where she was going (quite normal for me – I chat to birds, trees, and plants alike), and she froze, keeping close to the grass. I was able to move quite close to her as I weeded the beds and still she had kept her position, sitting there like a stone, pretending she wasn't there, and ignoring me. On a ploughed field nobody would know she was there but here, on lush green grass, she stood out like a sore thumb. As I moved on, she moved too, closer to the beds until she was on the opposite side to me. I had left her alone and thought nothing of it but was glad of the company. I often have pheasants wandering the garden, perched on a stump or resting in the undergrowth. It is good to see their array of colours as you peer out into the garden first thing in the morning.

Back to this morning, when I was pottering about with my herbs, digging them up to replant and pot up. To my amazement, I found four pheasant eggs in the corner of the bed I was working in. The hen pheasant had laid her eggs in amongst my marjoram, buried slightly under the soil, in an indentation. She has good taste and must have required a first-class nesting site that smelled fresh from morning 'til night.

Needless to say, I left the eggs and the clump of marjoram protecting them and now know what the bold hen pheasant was up to yesterday when she wouldn't budge from her position on the grass.

~

I've come in now for a welcome and reviving cup of coffee before I tackle another bed, but I am intrigued with the small mounds of gravel from the pathway, which have appeared at the side of the cottage. On inspection there is nothing under the mounds, and if I rake them away then they're back the next morning. I can only think that a hedgehog or a fox is rooting about looking for worms and slugs and, in their investigation, piles up the stones as they go.

I do have a hedgehog in the front garden and his little black calling cards have started to appear again now the weather is warming up. He lives in a clump of old fir-tree branches and dried leaves, which I leave there for him. However, when disturbed last year, while I was raking the continual fall of beech leaves, he was most disgruntled. My prickly, pretty-faced friend must have been out for a wander and I didn't expect to see him where I did. I must have poked him with my rake, for his little, black, beady nose appeared from out of the leaves, sniffing the air. His nose was very shiny and looked as if it had been polished with boot-blacking. Circling his head and assuming that all was good to go, he ambled out of the pile of leaves, some of which were still stuck to his prickles, and made his way back to his fir-tree home. I've not seen him since but wonder if he is making himself busy by re-designing my pathway for me.

However, we have a very beautiful fox in the vicinity too, who was greatly in evidence in the early hours of the morning some days ago. He is a stunning specimen in bright ginger colours, with a brush that any fox would be proud of, tipped with bright white at the end. I saw him on Sunday morning, passing by the gate, nose down, tail out straight behind him as he made his way across the lane and into the field opposite. I lost sight of him there, as a large beech tree blocks my view, and I suppose my gravel mounds could be down to him, too, although they are very delicately made.

As I type there are blue tits pecking around the window frame and the chaffinches are still calling non-stop. A great spotted woodpecker is favouring the garden table to sit on while deciding which nut feeder to visit. No matter which one he chooses, he will always cling to the side away from me, which is very frustrating sometimes. With a red spot on the back of his head I know he's a male, and with his bouncy flight he's off and away to the row of beech trees on the left of the garden. From the garden, I can quite distinctly hear him drumming away at the tree trunks, busy in his work, but he visits regularly and I'm happy to feed him and his family.

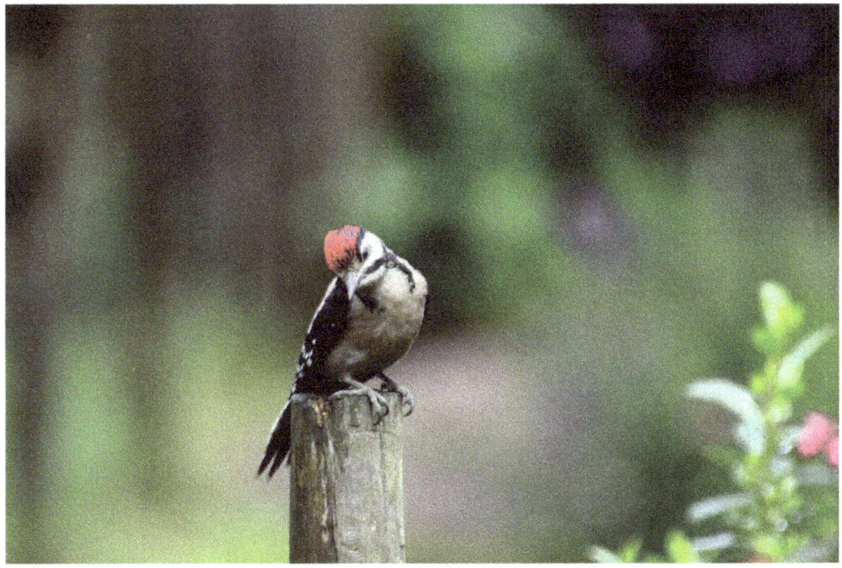

Coffee-break over, I must return to my herbs and the solace of the garden, hard though it is to resist the lemon drizzle cake sitting downstairs in my small but homely kitchen.

Red Deer Return

This is the sight that greeted me at half past six this morning, when I pulled back the curtains to let in the day.

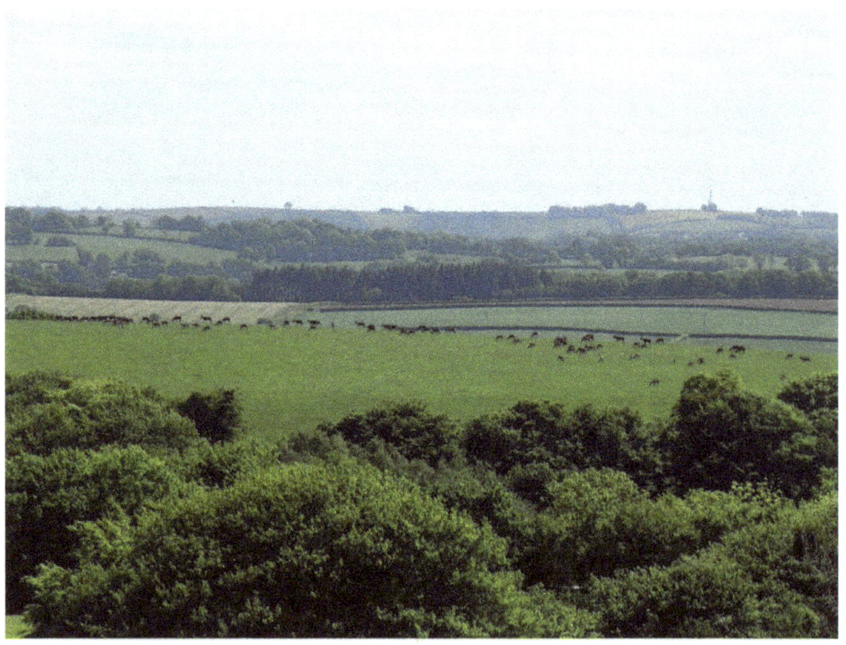

The red deer had returned to the field earlier than expected and I have never seen a herd so large. There were around 75–80 deer, grazing peacefully in the early morning sun, with a bright white mist hovering over them in the valley: a stunning view. It was strange to see them because they usually follow a pattern of around two weeks on and two weeks off, and they had only been gone from my view for a couple of days. I have to admit that I did let out a very tiny, "Wow," before I grabbed my camera. I then settled down, with a cup of Earl Grey and a chocolate digestive, to watch them for a while. An hour later they were still grazing, heads down.

I had been rudely awoken even earlier this morning – at around half past three – by a commotion out on the front lawn. With the moon in her dark phase, hidden from view, the room was pitch black. If I had held my hand in front of my face, I wouldn't have been able to see it for some minutes, but I'm used to the darkness and the solitary air it brings to the room. I guessed the sounds I could hear were a wily fox, out on the tiles, but I knew that I wouldn't be able to see anything, even if I went to investigate, so I lay waiting – in vain – for sleep to come to me once again.

The sounds of the countryside permeate the room most nights and I'll drift off amidst an orchestra of the weird and wonderful, but they don't usually wake me during the early morning hours. They're sounds that I love to hear, though: owls, sheep, cattle, foxes, tractors working late into the night, and, in the rutting season, the roaring of the red deer. There are no planes, trains, or buses (and only a very few cars) and I'm happy for it to be that way.

~

Yesterday evening I had been out trying to photograph a short-eared owl. I sat for an hour, with a coffee, in the location I'd seen it in a couple of days previously. It was high on the moor, with views that go on forever, and I was quite happy to sit and ponder for a while.

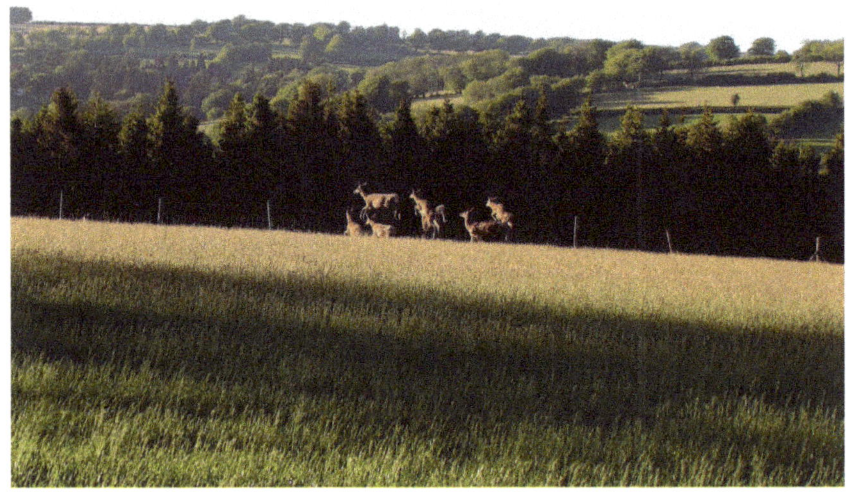

Over in a field, on the other side of a row of trees, I could see five or six deer grazing in the early evening sun. On my side of the trees was a lone hind, pottering about in a grassy oasis amongst the clumps of boggy sedge and grasses. She made no attempt to join the others and seemed content to keep her lush patch of grass to herself. As the evening wore on another herd appeared in a further field and, eventually, they joined ranks and became one.

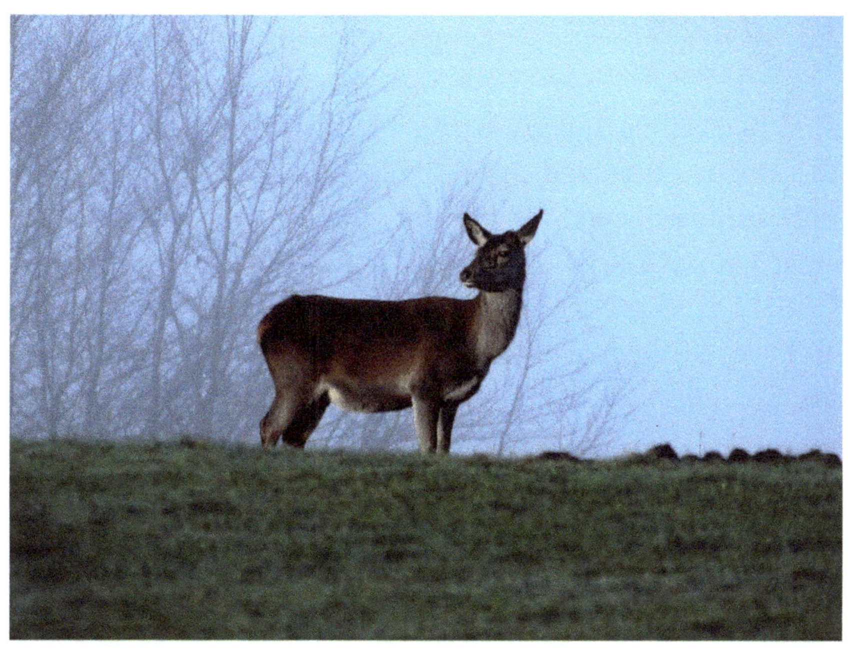

There was still no sign of the owl and I wondered if it had departed for its nesting grounds further north. I had the sheep to keep me company, though, and they wandered along in front of me, not bothering that I was there, cross-legged on a bank, sipping coffee. They passed me by, arrived at the end of the field, and came all the way back again, probably wondering why they'd bothered in the first place.

I watched as skylarks rose from the grass, in full song, their high-pitched, shrill notes continually gathering speed as they climbed, becoming a spot in the still, blue sky. Meadow pipits bobbed along the tops of the dried grasses, flitting up and down before coming to rest, and crows, shining bluey-black in the late sunshine, were outlined against the sky while clinging to the topmost branches of a close-by tree.

While sitting quietly there, I heard my first cuckoo of the season. It rattled off a dozen of its gentle calls in one rally and then again five minutes later. Both sounded quite close by, but I know from experience that's not always the case. Last year, I sat for many hours observing the cuckoos and one of them had the most peculiar song. It cuckooed like any cuckoo would, with the "koo" part sounding fine, but then it all went pear-shaped, with that last syllable sounding like a spring had come loose. It was like something out of a cartoon and quite funny to listen to – very distinctive though.

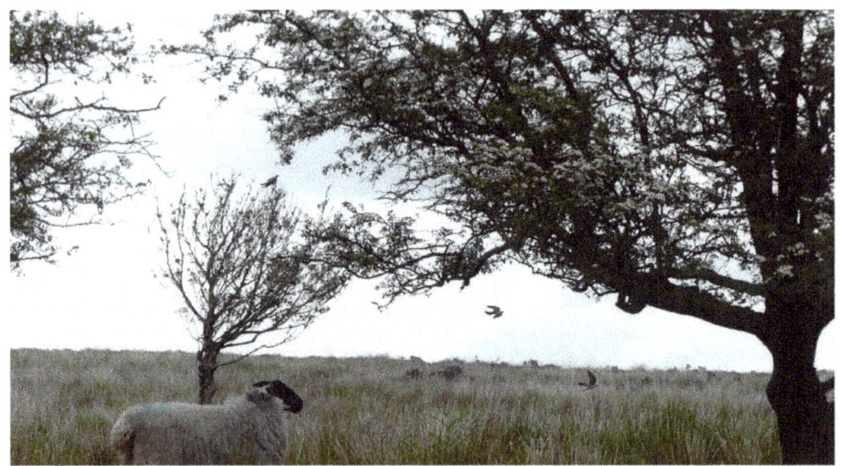

After an hour and a half of sitting on my bank I had seen many, many birds – but no owl. Deciding to move to a new location, I jumped back into the car, turned it around and made my way back whence I'd come. A group of deer were to my left, standing out like silhouettes against the horizon, so I stopped again and watched them while the sun began to sink away and out of sight.

Then, out of nowhere, I spotted the short-eared owl. Hovering above the grassland, it was very close to me but the sun was disappearing fast and I knew that my camera would struggle. Climbing onto the bank, I sat amongst the heather and moss and watched this beautiful bird, with its huge wingspan, hunting, turning this way and that, flying away from me and then returning to allow me another view. The owl was then joined by a second and, even though I was a little chilly now, I stayed sitting, enjoying the moment because I knew I may not get another chance before the owl was off and gone. In the last moments, one of the owls chased off a crow. Dipping and diving, it made its presence felt and then both disappeared from sight over the ridge.

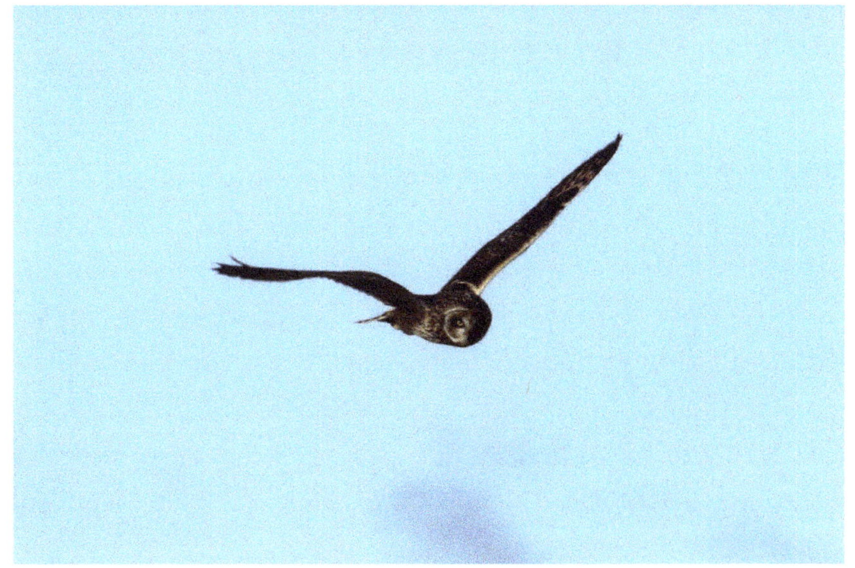

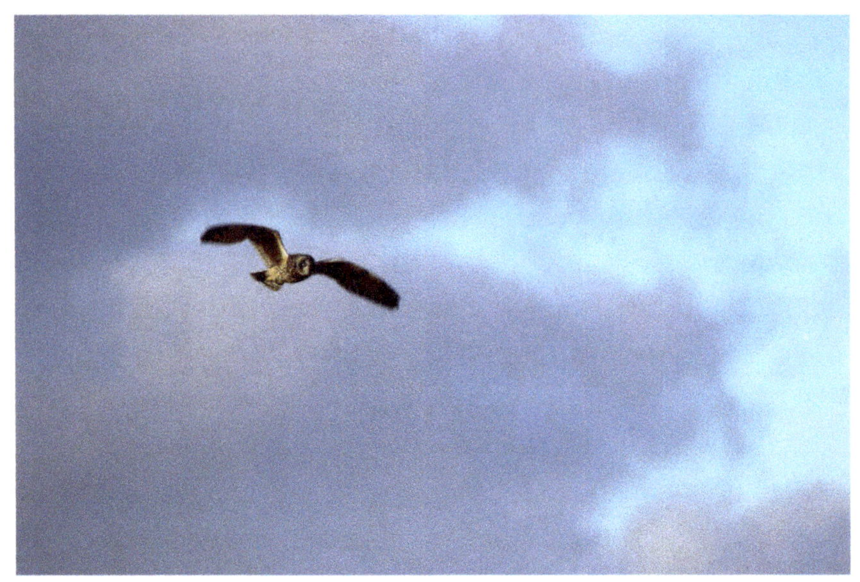

Wearily, I made my way back to the cottage for a cuppa and my bed. I was looking forward to a good night's sleep – and then my night time visitors woke me in the early hours and I've been awake since.

~

The deer have moved across the field now and are out of sight, apart from one lone stag who is standing and looking my way. Both his antlers are intact, with two and three atop, and the tips are glowing white in the morning sun. He's a stunning sight to behold as he starts to strut across the field to join the herd. The eerie morning mist has lifted, I can see into the distance beyond and across the fields, and I know it's going to be another warm day to fill with simple pleasures.

Simonsbath to Cow Castle

It's Sunday and I've been proper rambling this morning, but not the outdoor, walking, wandering type. No, I've been rambling on the telling bone for the last hour to my oldest and best friend of fifty-two years. We live miles apart and have done for many years but it's never stopped us being there for each other. Spending an hour out of my day to laugh like a drain, chat about our small grandsons and reminisce is a small price to pay for starting out later than expected on a morning ramble along the river. We always giggle like the teenagers we once were – it's so good for the soul to share and laugh. We've shared many a wander, too, in our lives, both emotionally and on foot.

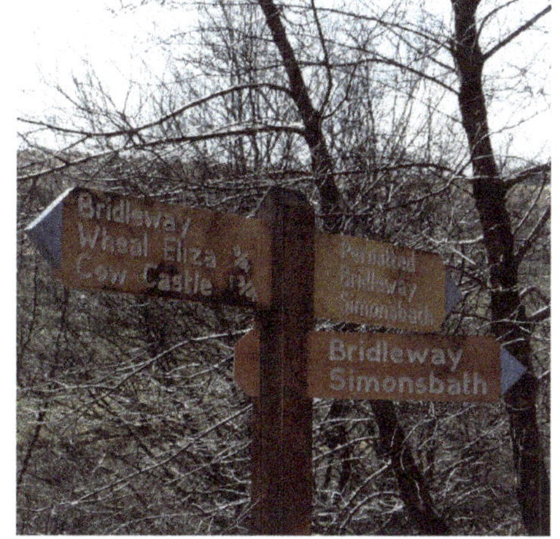

Today, after saying goodbye, eventually, I am on my own and a-rambling I will go, after a bacon sarnie and a cup of Earl Grey. As I watch the birds at the feeders, from my kitchen window, I can see the vibrancy in their feathers now they are mating and nesting, especially the brave little blue tits. It's good to see a pair of goldfinches back for another year, as they nest in the rhododendrons at the front of the house. It's peaceful out there in the lane for them, and I have the added bonus of being able to see them from the bedroom window while drinking my early morning cuppa.

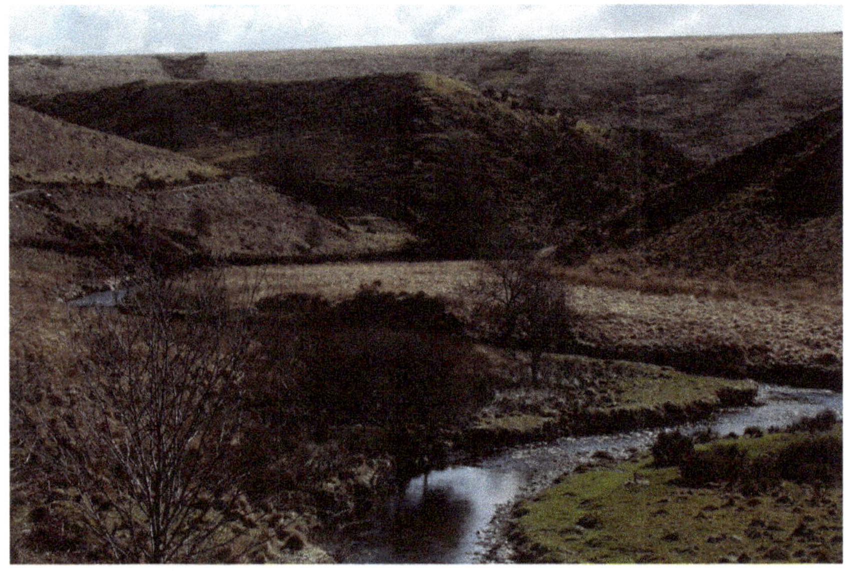

I've decided today to wander along the River Barle from Simonsbath. It's quite a glorious day and I'm looking forward to seeing the sunlight reflecting on the river as I walk. So, donning my Bear Grylls charity shop fleece (don't know how I ever managed without it!) I'm off and up the road. The moor looks as if it's been bleached in the sunlight and it seems to shimmer as the grasses move in the gentle breeze. Exmoor ponies graze around the thorn trees, backs still to the breeze, but enjoying the welcome break from the recent wet days. Two of them cross the road in front of me. It's always worthwhile stopping to admire them when out and about.

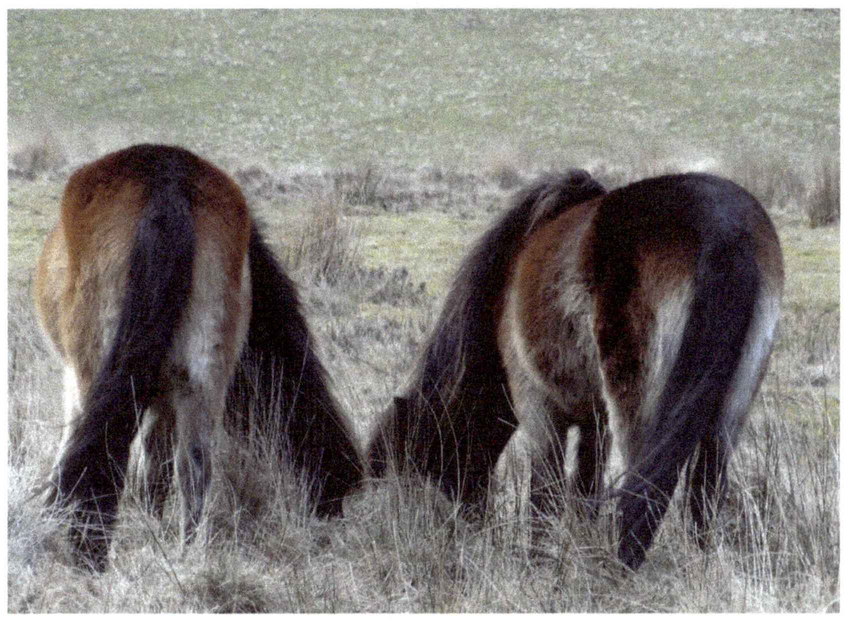

At Birchcleave Wood I join the newly laid path that follows the stunning Barle as it winds itself through the valley in a twisting, turning fashion. It's full of character, wherever you choose to join it, and always a firm favourite of mine. I'm headed for Cow Castle. It's not a new haunt – I've been many times before – but it has a certain peaceful quality and the walk is never dull.

I try to remind myself that Simonsbath is situated at the centre of what once was the Royal Forest of Exmoor, that back as far as the 1500s, Simonsbath was simply a criss-cross of tracks over this beautiful, wild, and sometimes bleak moorland of ours. Walking this part of the moor, you can easily find yourself back in those days, with a little imagination. If only the moors could talk, I'm sure they'd have more than a few tales to tell about the residents back then.

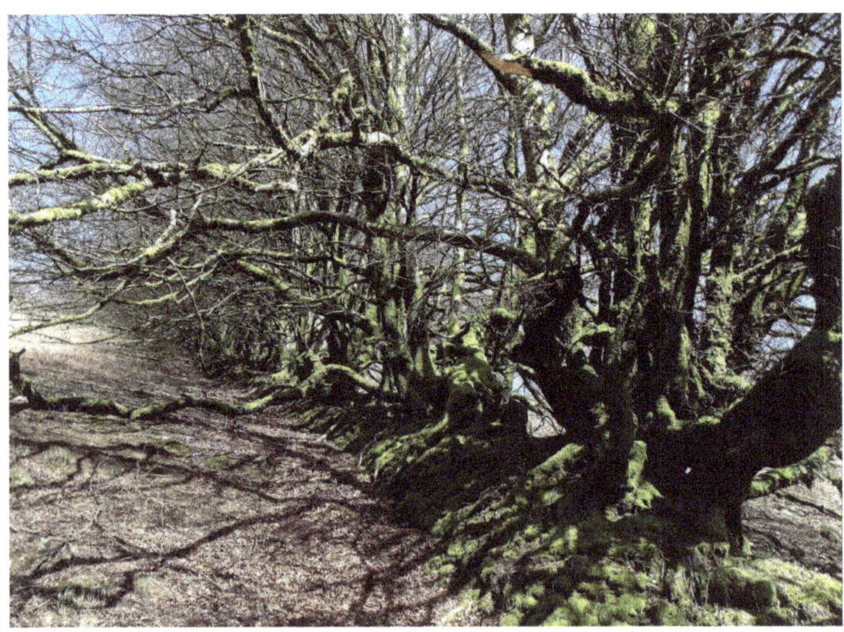

Trees are plentiful at the beginning of the path, as I'm passing Birchcleave Wood on my left. It's said to be the highest beech wood in the country and, whether it is or not, there are some wonderful shapes to behold. I love to witness the trees at this time of year, just before the leaves burst from their buds, as you can really see into the heart of the branches and wonder at their skeletal structure. It's also an excellent opportunity to see the many birds that flit back and forth from the woodland to the meadow as I wander. The pathway opens out, leaving the woodland behind, with just the odd tree hanging on. But there are still the wonderful ancient lines of beech to be seen here and there before leaving them behind for gorse, bracken, and marshland grasses.

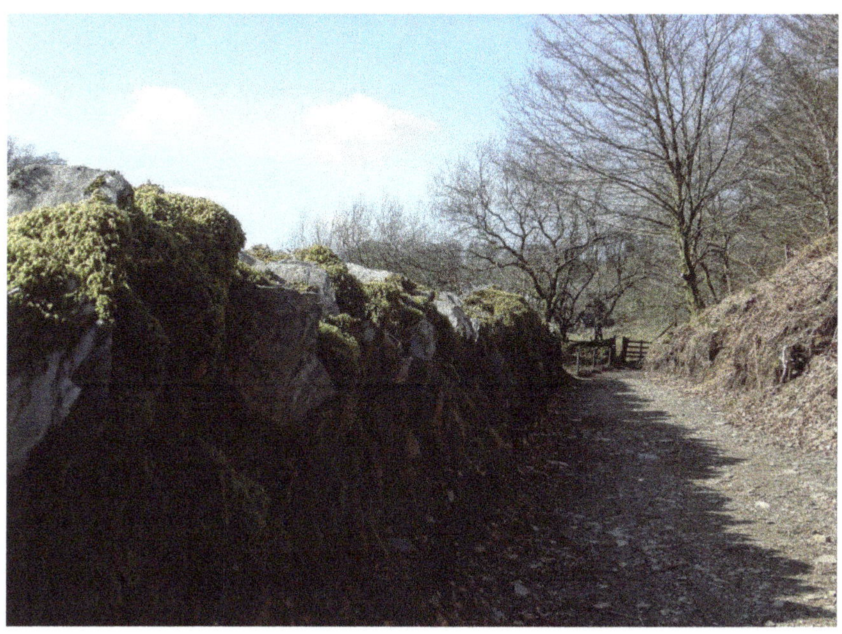

The Exmoor National Park Authority (ENPA) have done a grand job of re-laying the pathway and it's not as undulating as it was on previous visits. However, the character of the walk is still evident as the path follows the meandering great Barle river, making its way on to Landacre Bridge. On either side are hills which rise dramatically towards the sky and, as you wander, you feel as if you're being cushioned by these huge natural mounds.

They reach down from the sky and tempt you to walk to the next bend – further and further. Who knows what you'll find as you round the next corner?

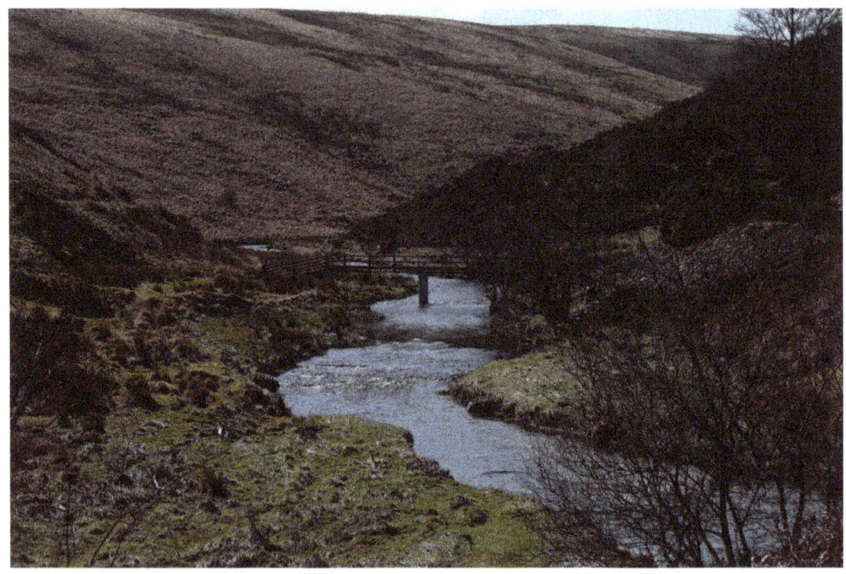

Greens and browns in abundance, with smatterings of yellow, paint the perfect picture for me: Exmoor is at its very best at this time of year. Sometimes you'll lose sight of the river as you round a bend or make the climb to a rise, but it's not for long and you know it's there – you can hear it! I can lose myself in my thoughts as I walk this route, the track taking me up a little and then dropping me down again, following in the wake of the many sheep that graze this area.

I always keep my eyes open for wildlife as I walk and today I come across a slow worm, sunning itself on this beautifully warm day, just off the pathway. Its body glows golden brown in the sunlight and I kneel down to take a closer look and, hopefully, encourage it to move into cover and off the pathway, with just a look and silent plea from me.

The slow worm evokes childhood memories for me as silky feeling creatures, such as snakes and the like, are of no worry to me. I used to keep two grass snakes as a youngster. They were never kept indoors but happily lived in the garden, by our fishpond. I would carry them with me, in my pocket, when shopping with my mum or playing out and, as I kept a toad on me, too, people thought me strange; they never knew what I'd produce from any part of my clothing, at any given time. I had a wonderful childhood!

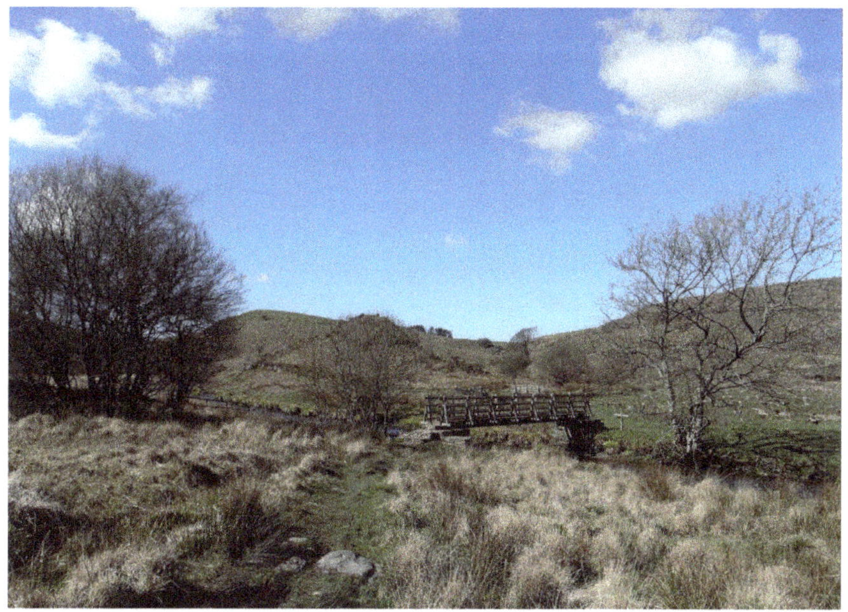

Passing Flex Barrow and tramping on towards Wheal Eliza, the mine ruins, I sit for a while and look across the river. I remember a time when I walked this way at the end of summer. The riverside was awash with orange and green as crocosmia flowered profusely, dangling and swaying into the flowing water. So many colour palettes can be found on Exmoor and each and every one of them different as the seasons change. No area stays the same as we travel through spring, summer, autumn, and winter – and that's why the moor is loved by so many.

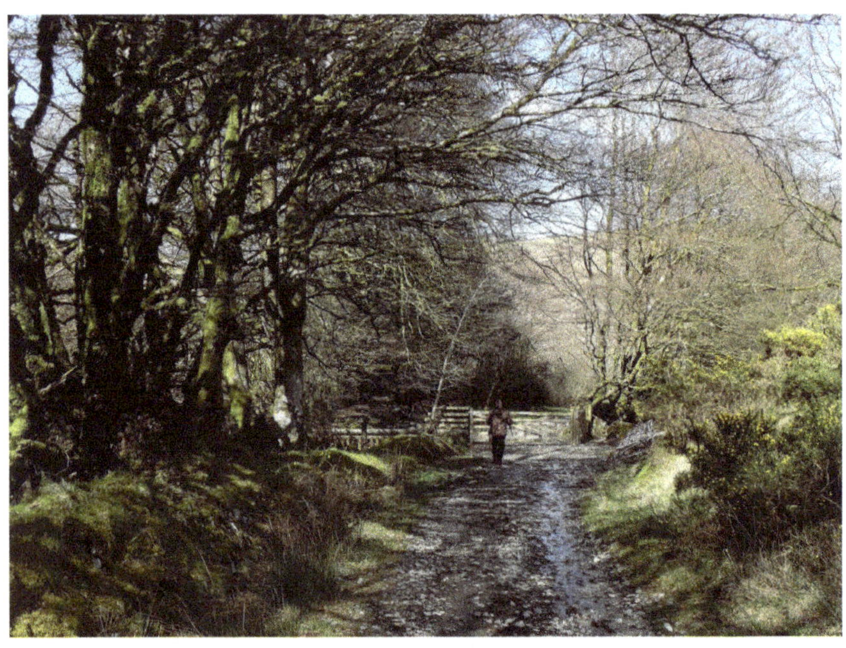

I cut through a hedge-bank on the left – it's a beech hedge, gnarled, and full of history – and now find myself walking along the river once more. It's greener here and has flattened out somewhat. It's peaceful, enchanting and, stepping through the beech hedge, I feel as if I've popped into a different world by simply traversing a hedgerow. However, I find I've nearly reached my destination: the hillock on which Cow Castle sits. To fully appreciate where I've wandered this fine day, I need to walk a little further to see the rise of Great Ferny Ball. I also get to view the wooden bridges that cross the river and which would take me up towards Horsen Farm – but that's for another day.

Having crossed the small wooden bridge spanning the river here, I've come into a clearing. There is evidence of more work done by the ENPA and I can rest for a while, and partake of my apple and bag of crisps, on one of the tree stumps. To the left of me is Cow Castle and to the right is open ground which rises to Great Ferny Ball. I am sorely tempted to walk on, over the bridge, across the boggy, damp grass, and through the gate towards a further bridge, but know I should be making my way home again. Instead I sit, eyes skyward, watching a lone buzzard circling and dipping and diving over the wonderful landscape I'm part of.

Just across the way is a ford, primarily used by horses. The river is so very clear and clean; watching it flow and tumble over the stones and boulders is spellbinding and, even though I am fully aware that time is passing by, I have to perch on a ready-made step, legs dangling over the water, and watch as the water passes on by. Time to retrace my steps and I turn a circle, taking in my quiet surroundings. I nod my thanks to the moor, steeped in history and character, for being able to be part of it in my lifetime.

I wish I could bottle the emotions and feelings that I have when I walk so that others, caught up in the rat race of life, could experience what I do: peace and utter joy at being out in the open with my thoughts, away from the humdrum of what life throws at us on a daily basis. This, out here, is freedom of a very special kind. I wish my friend of fifty-two years could be with me now so that she could experience it too, or that I could pop her a bottle of my 'emotion potion' in the post so we could share yet another memory together in the years to come. This book is the next best thing.

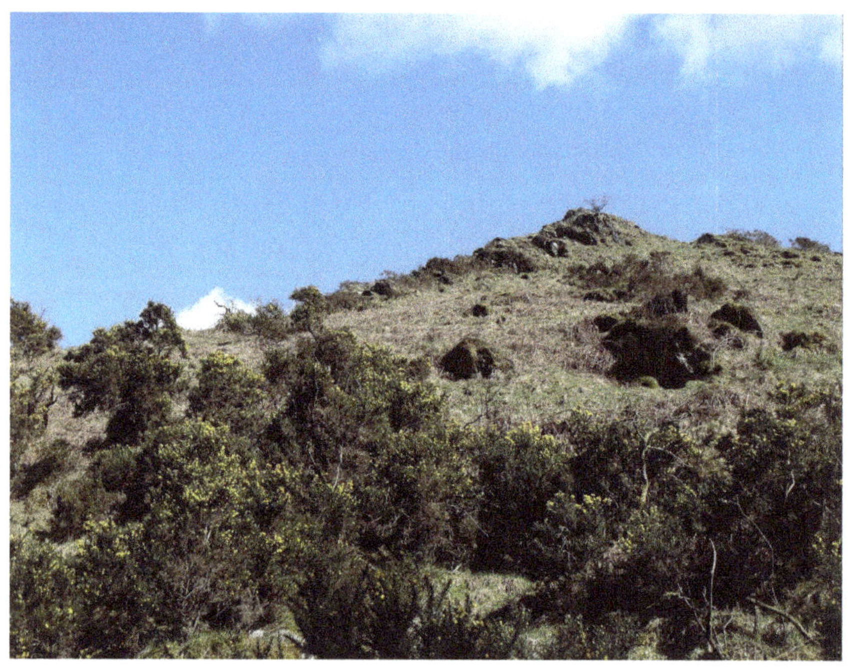

So it's homeward bound for me then and, perhaps, a half of cider at the Exmoor Forest Inn. Simple pleasures.

Babysitting, Birds, Badgers, and Back Home

I've been away. Some would say 'away with the fairies' and, surprisingly, I wouldn't argue with that. However, I've really been away – from home, from Exmoor, and for the whole of last week. It's been bittersweet; I was away because my daughter and little grandson needed me and, without a second's thought, I was there for them both, but time away from the cottage is always hard for me to deal with. My daughter understands the passion I have for the place where I live; she understands that my life here on Exmoor is entwined with the land outside my windows and the home that I am so much a part of. My excuse is that I'm a true Cancerian in every aspect: a family-loving home-bird who hates change. But I am a mother-figure personified, in every sense, so I toddled off for a week on the Wirral … but now I'm back and, as the song goes, I'm feeling good!

On arriving home I had to beat a pathway to my back door through an explosion of weeds which had, once again, shot up in my absence. Turn your back and all that … But I decided to deal with those later. My garden had exploded, too, and was a mass of colour, which looked quite professionally planned on first glance but to my 'trained' eye it's all very haphazard and chaotic – just the way I like it.

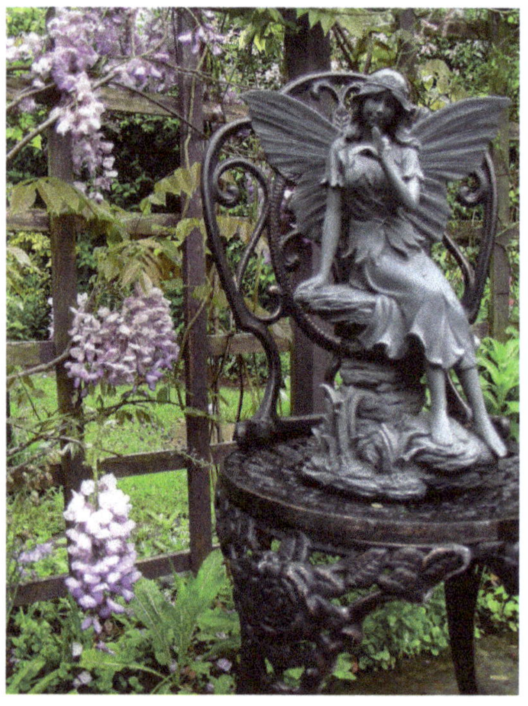

My stone-and-slate steps up to the main garden were covered in lilac blossom and my fingers itched to take the broom and begin sweeping. I always have a broom outside the back door because when I sweep, I think. I find it's good therapy and very relaxing to take a broom and rhythmically sweep away not only whatever is on the ground, but my own troubles and thoughts too. (You see? I *am* away with the fairies more often than I let on.) However, what really needed doing was seed-sowing, so I headed to my veg beds.

I was sat sowing radish seeds when, to my amazement, the chattering of a swallow made me look up. It was very loud and very close by and I turned my head towards the sound. Behind me, sitting perched on my bean poles, was a lone swallow. It was about four feet away and carried on chittering away as I watched it, watching me. Swift as ever, the clever birds were diving for small insects as 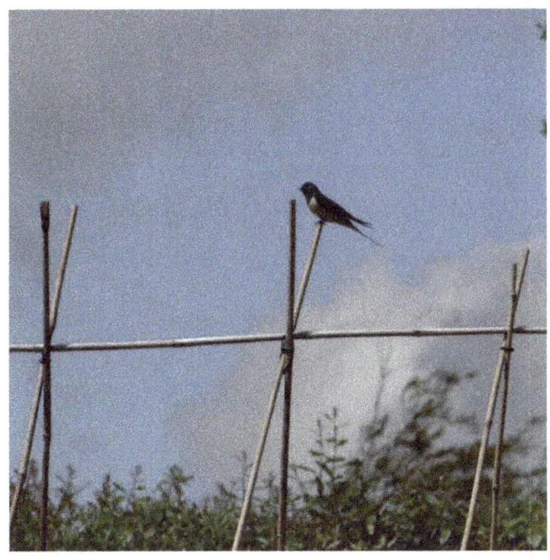 I turned over the earth and were working in close proximity to me, following me up the paddock as I worked in the beds. I must have been slacking in my work for this one to sit, waiting on my bean pole struts, for me to turn the soil once again. In that moment, it was so good to be home.

However, the rain we've had this morning (and it's been torrential) has flattened out the scented geranium clumps, assisted the taller foxgloves in falling to one side, and has probably drowned and washed away the seeds I'd planted in my raised beds yesterday. It's still going on now but it's all quite promising for this afternoon so onwards and upwards we go.

Having been woken this morning, at around half past six, by the dulcet tones of a lone blackbird, I opened my eyes and felt utter contentment. Then without further ado the song turned into panic-stricken cluck-clucking as an emergency was declared by the soloist outside the bedroom window. The dastardly magpie had probably struck again and was after the blackbird's eggs or young.

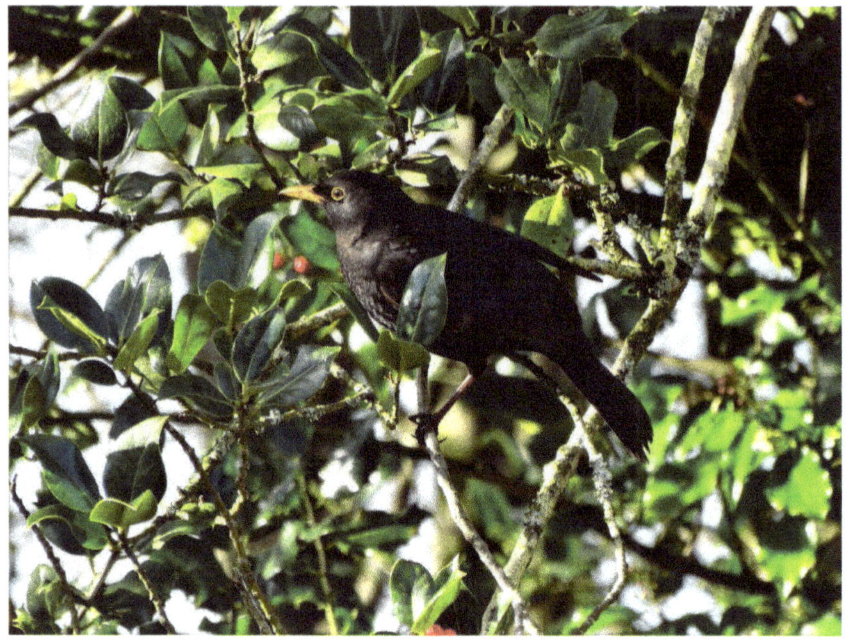

Magpies are notorious for attacking birds in the garden. They'll think nothing of taking out a blue tit or two but are not strictly carnivorous – one took several leaves of a little gem lettuce from the bird table the day before yesterday. I'd only just put the leaves out, thinking that the finches may have a peck or two from them. I turned my back to peg some washing on the line, came back down the steps and the leaves were gone! All of them … vanished into thin air.

Needing to know who had taken them in such a short space of time, I replenished the bird table and sat by the kitchen window to watch. Down came the magpie and off went the lettuce, dangling from the magpie's beak, like an extra wing. With no trouble at all, it took the lot; perhaps it had a nice three-bean salad to go with it for lunch that day; who knows?

After planting out some of my home-grown herbs, filling gaps in my banked-up flower bed where I'd thinned out the lungwort, I thought I'd wander down across the fields towards the woodland. The sun was out, it wasn't too warm as the breeze was chill but it would do me good to be upright instead of bent over on my knees tilling the earth.

I'd grabbed some crackers and cheese, an apple and some fruit pastilles, and was gone before anything could change my mind, like the housework, more weeding … ironing even.

Since I'd been home I'd already reaffirmed my connection with this special part of the world, so I'd already been walkabout. I needed to feel the ground beneath my feet, the air on my skin, and the sun on my back. However, the most important job to be done was to cleanse my necklace, bracelet, and rings in the clear waters of an Exmoor river and that couldn't wait, hence the hurry to be out and about.

This wander would take me down to the woods where we knew there to be a new badger sett. It was at the bottom of a meadow-like field, on the edge of the wood and we'd had our eye on it for some time. There had been excavation going on for some weeks and, little by little, the hole leading underground had become larger and wider. Around the entrance there was a wonderful mound of earth, mixed with small stones and rocks of a type that you'll find anywhere if you dig around these parts. Even my garden is full of them and it's a bane when you're trying to plant something quickly.

It was here that I was headed – not a long walk but long enough to appease my appetite for being out on the moor and to work up a foody appetite too. The walk down to the woodland had always inspired me to stop awhile, take in the breathtaking view and revel in the fact that I live here and, unlike the unfortunate visitors to Exmoor who have to return home at the end of their stay, I simply have to walk (maybe trudge) back up the hill and there I be.

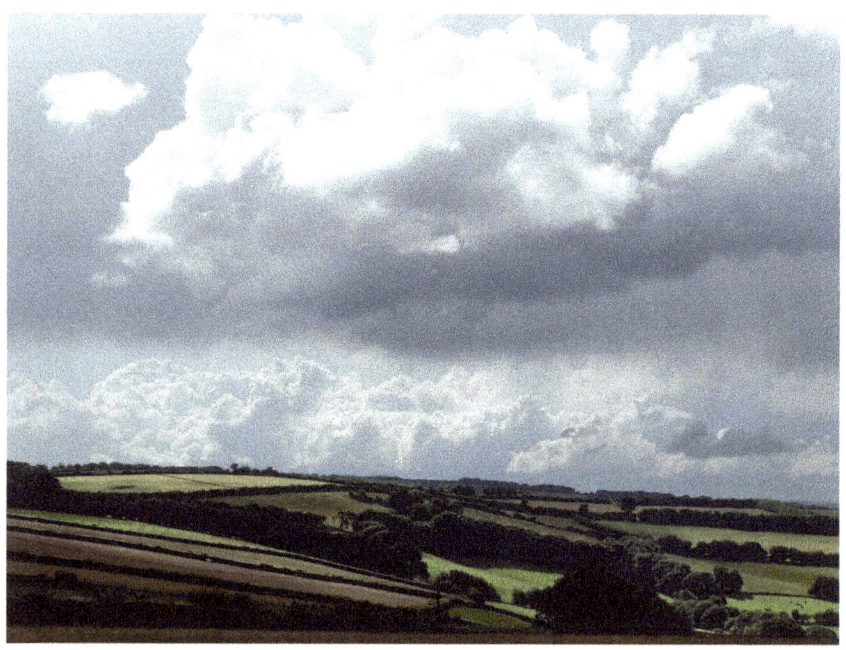

I have never taken for granted the fact that I live here, because I know how blessed I am.

Lush fields took my feet towards an ancient hedgerow where a makeshift stile helped me over the obstacle. A wren called out with its huge song as I stepped up and over

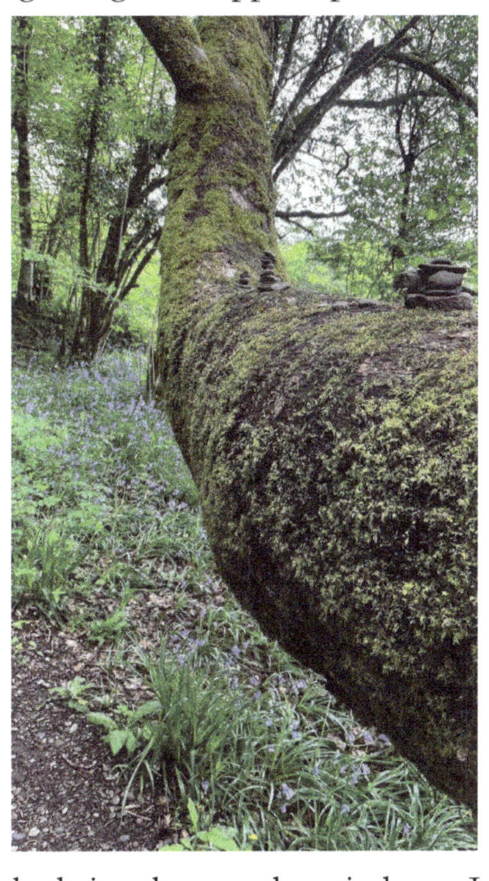

into the next field, but I still listened as I walked through a meadow of wild flowers and grasses. Cuckoo flower, yellow buttercups, blue speedwell, and tufty balls of red clover all sang to me as I wandered the outskirts of this friendly expanse of green.

I could see the woods now – tall fir trees reaching to the blue sky above but flanked by old beech trees, full of leaf and swaying in the breeze. They shushed and hushed in the gentle wind as I approached them. It's a sound that fills my ears most days as my own garden is edged with beech trees. Without pulling back the curtains, I can usually tell what weather is waiting for me outside, simply by listening to what the trees are imparting with their voices.

From here I could see the river, far below, meandering along. I knew that there would be walkers enjoying the pathway alongside it, yet they had no idea that I was up in the wood that day. I wanted the badgers to have no idea I was there either, if that was at all possible. I wanted a position above the sett to see if there had been any developments and this meant that I had to pass it via the woodland. I skirted wide through the trees, after using a sturdy wooden gate to enter the woods.

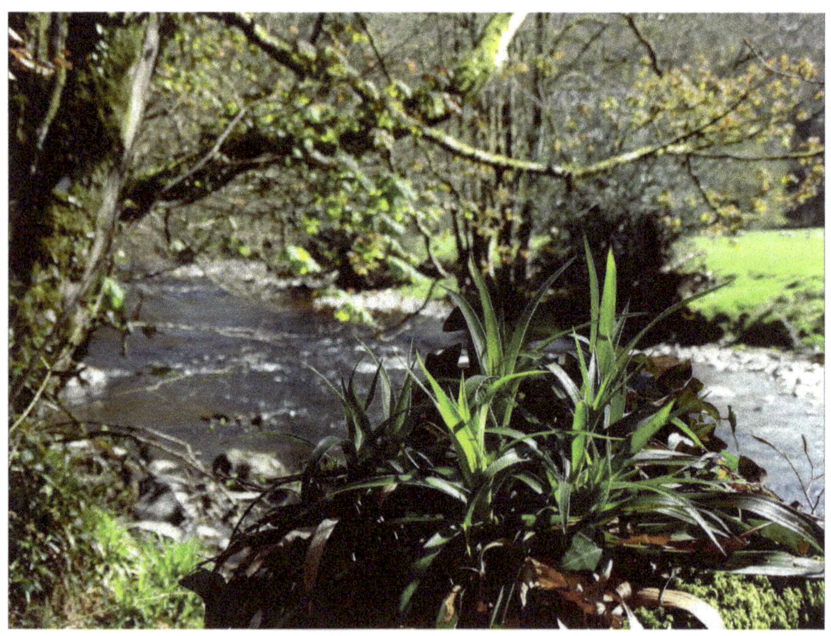

From my viewpoint, and with my trusty binoculars, I could see that the entrance to the sett had collapsed but on the other side of a low fence another entrance had been dug. Again, there was a huge mound of the tell-tale earth, complete with small stones, outside the opening. I was pleased to see this as it showed the badgers hadn't abandoned their home but had simply patched it up and made good of it. This must surely be a good place for them to make their home: woodland, fields, and safety. The signs were there – trails to and from the sett, patches of grass dug up all over an adjoining field, a gap in the fence where the ground had worn flat, giving them access to and from their home. I was excited at what I was seeing and made my way back to the nearest field.

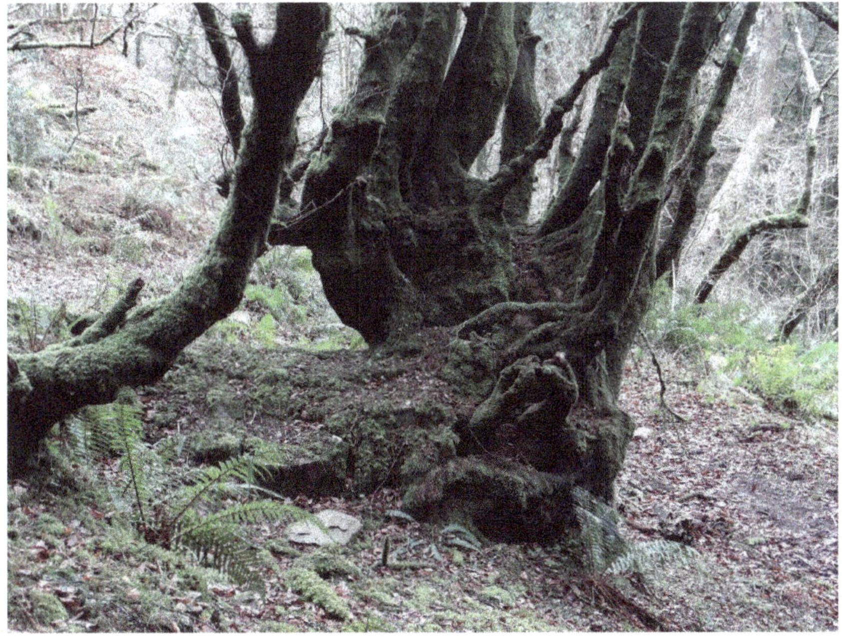

As has been proved on so many occasions, you never know what will emerge. So I sat with my camo coat on and a netting camo cover for my head, fairly well hidden, as I ate my make-do lunch. If I'm honest, I didn't expect to see anything that day but the temptation to sit for a while and bring my thoughts together had been too much of a lure. What better way than to spend a couple of hours taking in the silence and the peacefulness of the countryside, after a week away, looking at roof tops and dealing with clogged roads.

As I sat, a cheeky jay bounced down onto a nearby fence post, bold as brass. I'd seen it before, several times, in this neck of the woods, but today its plumage was vibrant against the backdrop of dark fir trees. It bounded backwards and forwards from floor to post for several minutes and then was gone.

The sound of twigs snapping on the woodland floor hit my ears. In the stillness of the day, this simple sound could be heard loud, sharp and clear. No wonder the red deer can pick us out when we're trying to creep about, thinking that we're being the world's best stalker! I wondered if it were red deer approaching to feast on the newly grown grass in the field – a usual spot for them to come and feed.

Keeping my head down I waited and watched, my heart beating louder, I was sure. But nothing appeared from out of the trees. A pheasant then, perhaps? As I sat, I cast my mind back to the last time I'd made my way down there to sit and watch, just before my week away. It had been barely dusk and I'd only come out for a quick wander with no intention to stay. But Exmoor does funny things to you and it urges you to wait a little while longer, then a little while longer still … until it's time you were off and away and in your bed.

Today, however, I needed the solace and was happy to just sit. You see, Exmoor comes and wraps its arms around you and doesn't let you forget how lucky you are to live here. It gives you peace and time to contemplate. But, as I always say, it's simple pleasures and moments like this that brings me so many smiles and that's what makes my day. You have to go out to see, go out to find, and it made me think … maybe I should have ventured further afield, when I was away last week, because everywhere holds special moments – if you take the time to look.

Another Side to Me

The rising sun woke me early this morning as it tried desperately to shine through the window. I gave it a helping hand by drawing the curtains and welcoming the day.

There were no deer in the fields this morning so I guess they've moved on to pastures new for a couple of weeks. They seem to stay around for roughly two weeks at a time and then they're gone. But they'll be back, working their way across the field in the opposite direction. I always miss seeing the herd but I know they'll return soon.

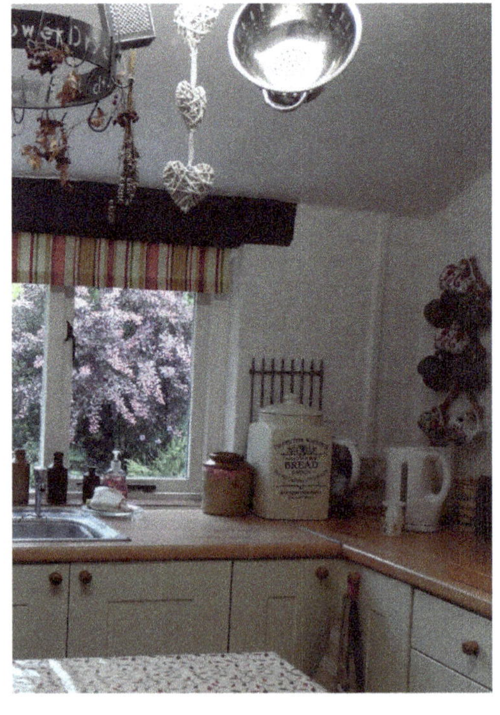

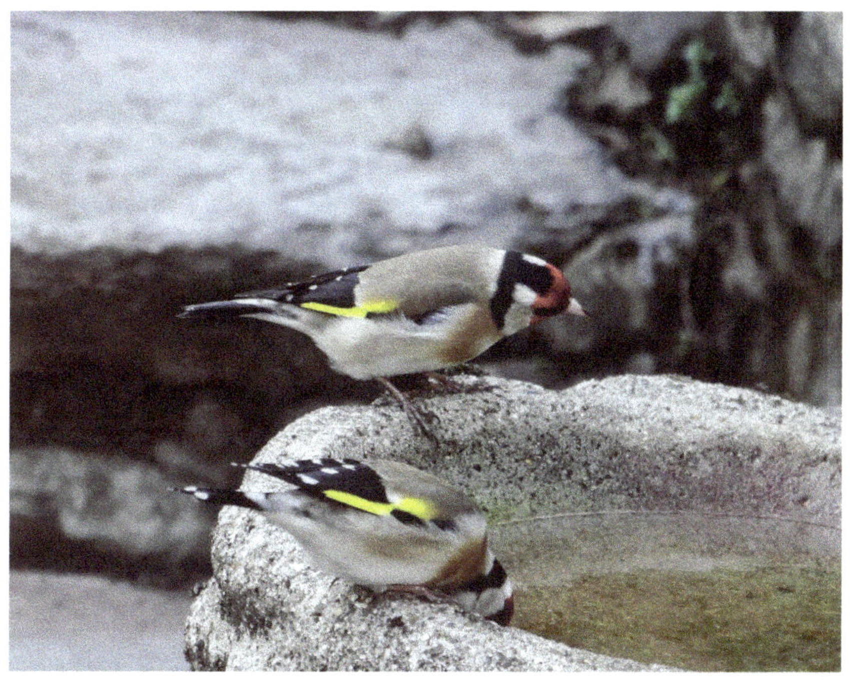

Great news though: I have a pair of goldfinches nesting in the front hedge! I'll be able to watch their antics from the bedroom window with my morning cuppa. I sat, with tea and toast, and watched them yesterday morning, flying in and out with beaks full of grass, feathers, and anything else they could find. They've certainly been very busy but they do have a good restaurant around the corner to replenish their energy. I really hope these pretty little finches stay around; it will be amazing to watch them.

My early start this morning meant that I managed to finish my chores in record time, so I took an early morning wander along the lane to watch the new lambs, who were full of beans! Lambs' tails were flicking and trembling as they ran about, leaping and jumping in their little lamb groups. If there's a mound in the field, then there's fantastic fun to be had at being King of the Castle. I could stay here awhile but need to get back so that I can bake for the weekend – and there's still weeding to be done, too, while the weather is being kind.

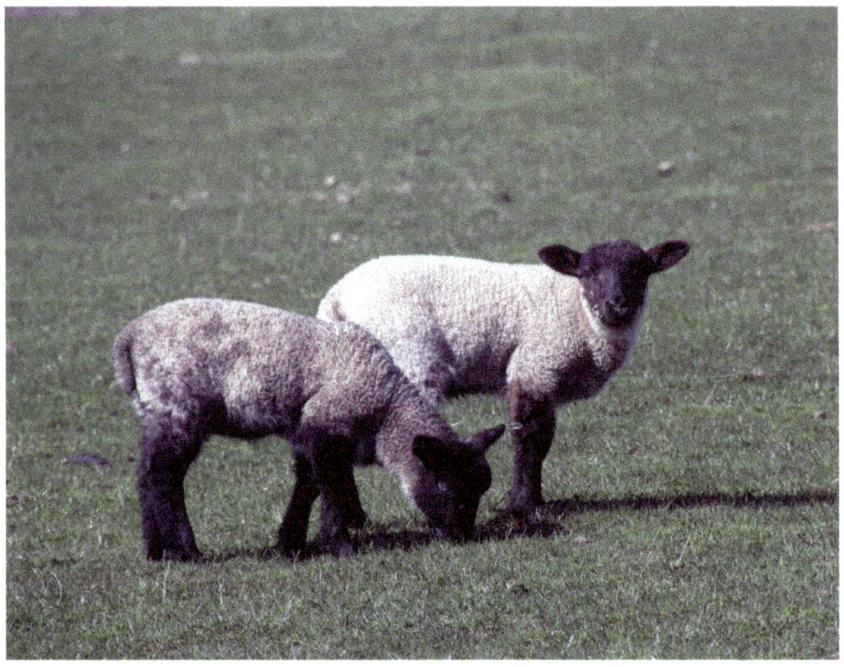

As there's not been a lot of baking going on just lately, (I'll blame that on the weather and not me being lazy) I need to throw a Victoria sponge together and get it in the oven first. My kitchen here at the cottage isn't large but it's very serviceable. Everything has a place and there seems to be a place for everything. It looks out over the bird table, its feeders and the garden, so my eyes are usually flitting thereabouts while I cook. The electric whisk can certainly be heard by visitors to the bird table but they seem to be used to it now, with the exception of the collared doves. They are lily-livered when it comes to noise or the tea towel flapping about, and movement in general.

The cottage is in a perfect spot, as the back door has a pretty decent vista too. It looks out onto a proper Exmoor bank complete with a stone wall, and all in the confines of the garden. The bank has delicate primroses growing on it, dwarf daffodils, forget-me-nots, and other greenery so whichever way I stand in the kitchen I feel like I'm outdoors. In the summer months the bank is overhung with fragrant shrubs. The warm mornings will welcome me with the smell of vanilla-scented mock orange and the heady scent of lilac.

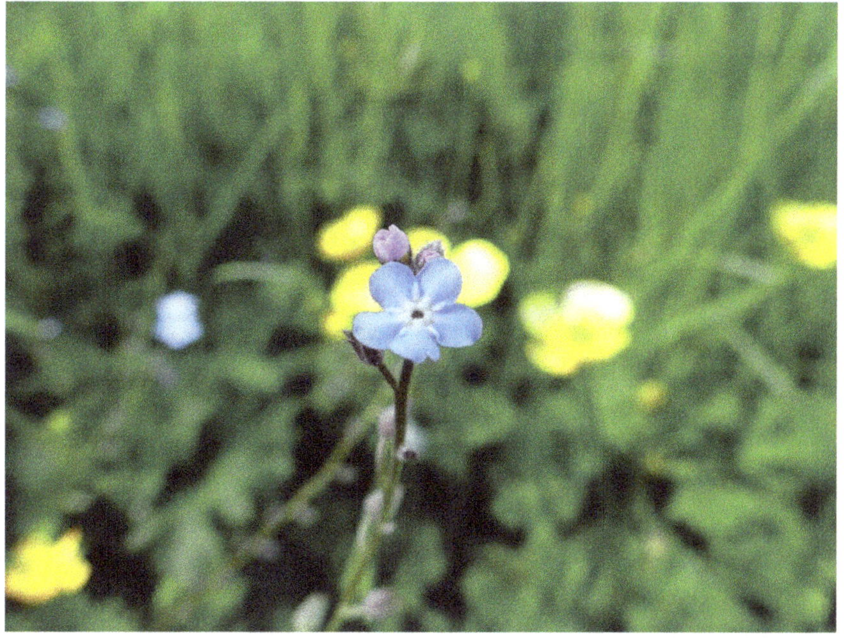

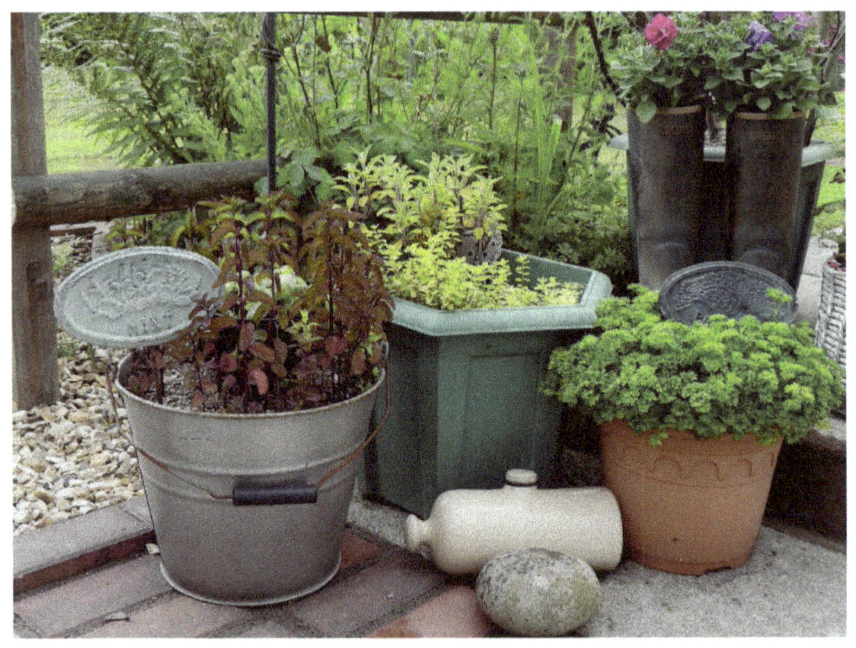

My kitchen has an old country feel to it with a hanging rail above the small table, where my pots are hung. You'll find a herb ring hanging there, too, where I dry herbs and flowers for use at a later date. It's not a modern kitchen by any means but it is full of love and cooking smells most of the time, so very homely. There's always something on the go, whether it be a cake, biscuits, bread, scones, quiche, creamy rice pudding, chicken pie, a simple jacket potato or delicious homemade soup: it's what makes my kitchen special to me. Even the postman puts his head in the door to tell me that something smells good! Delivery drivers are always offered a piece of cake to send them on their way; it's how I was raised and I'd like to keep the tradition going as long as I can. It's probably a very old-fashioned thing to do these days but my offer of cake has always been received with a smile and has yet to be refused. I always strive to do something for others, to make their day a little easier, no matter how small the gesture. If I can make a person smile then I've done a good job, for a smile or a kind word costs nothing.

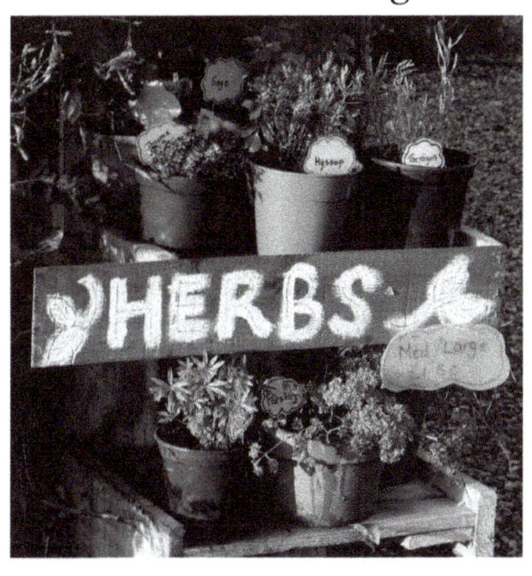

With a cake in the oven and some cheese scones waiting their turn, I started the clearing up. It's at times like this, when I'm alone and staring at the bubbles in the sink, that I wonder where the time has gone. Today is the anniversary of my dad's passing and that was twenty-six years ago. Where did the years go to? They fair fly past and I cannot drum into my children enough, to make the most of their lives and their children. Blink and they'll be gone! (The years, not the children.)

My mum is close by when I bake because she enjoyed baking, too, and she's probably telling me to stop dolly-daydreaming and take the cake out of the oven! I do this with some haste, replacing it with the scones and a rise in oven temperature. Before long the cheese scones are done and cooling on the rack, along with the cake. I hive one away to eat warm with a cup of Earl Grey, because I can't ignore the smell of a freshly baked scone. I'd like to say that I spread a little butter on the halved scone but that might just be stretching the truth a tad. A scone without plenty of butter is like a book without words.

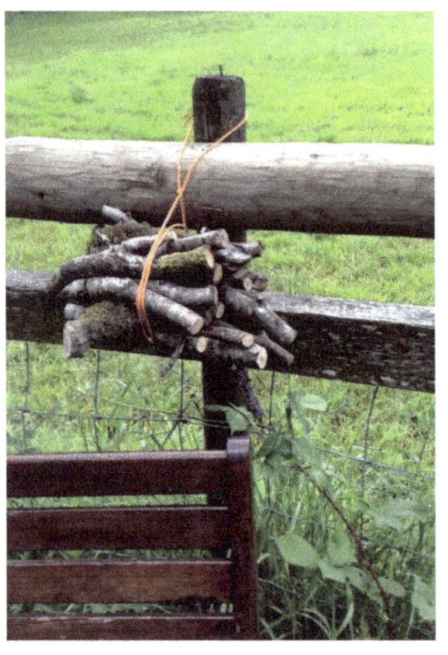

Scone and tea in hand, I wander up the old slate steps to the garden. Full of cracks and crevices, the steps spill over with primroses to the side and the promise of lady's mantle and sweet woodruff in the coming months. From my aged wooden bench I'm able to look across the moor, listen to the tractors working, and look to the gate when the horses pass by, which is several times a day. The clip-clop of their hooves on tarmac or the thud of them cantering up the field is a magnet to me, and it's not very often I resist going to stand at the gate to watch them pass by. It's Exmoor life and a childhood memory. The garden is a haven for me.

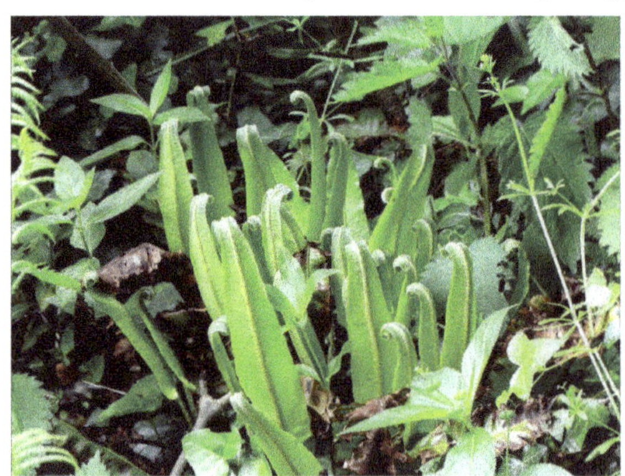

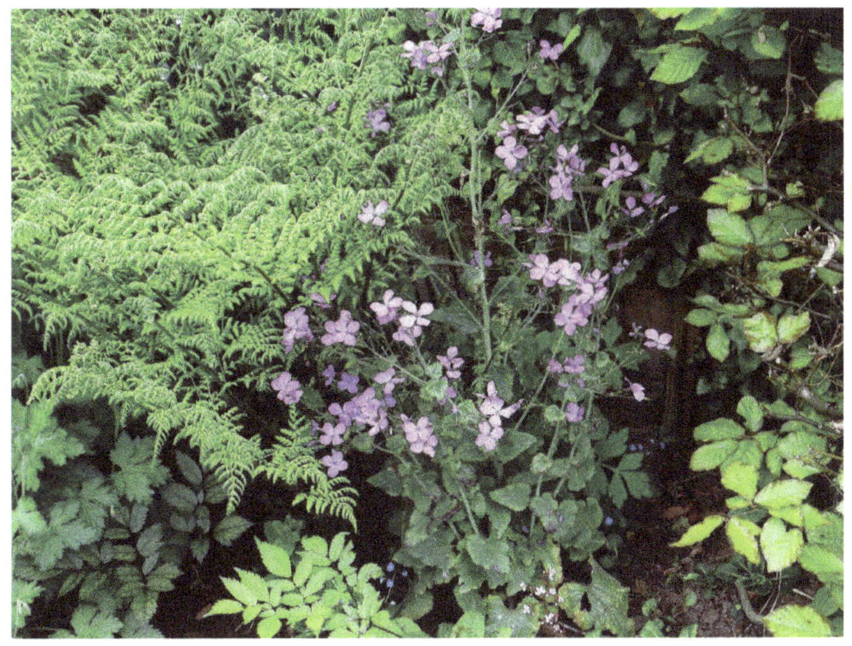

When I chat about weeding, I don't weed as such, pulling out every intruder I see. Most weeds give us extremely pretty flowers so I'm quite selective in what I remove. It's the invasive weeds that are unwelcome but perhaps 'unwelcome' is the wrong word as even some of those are really attractive in their foliage and flower. Wild flowers are often seen as weeds, too, by some, but they're never removed from my garden. Red campion, buttercups, swaying grasses, cow parsley, herb Robert all flow from the hedgerows, spilling over into the garden along with the plants and flowers that have been lovingly raised by me from seed. I use plants, wild flowers, herbs, and weeds a great deal in everyday life for one thing or another. It's another reason why I leave them to grow away happily as I never know when I'll need them. I'll always leave a thistle or two growing safely around the perimeter, as there is no greater protection for your garden, and life in general, than the presence of a good old thistle. Nettles too: an invasive plant, but an absolute necessity for butterflies, so they have a place.

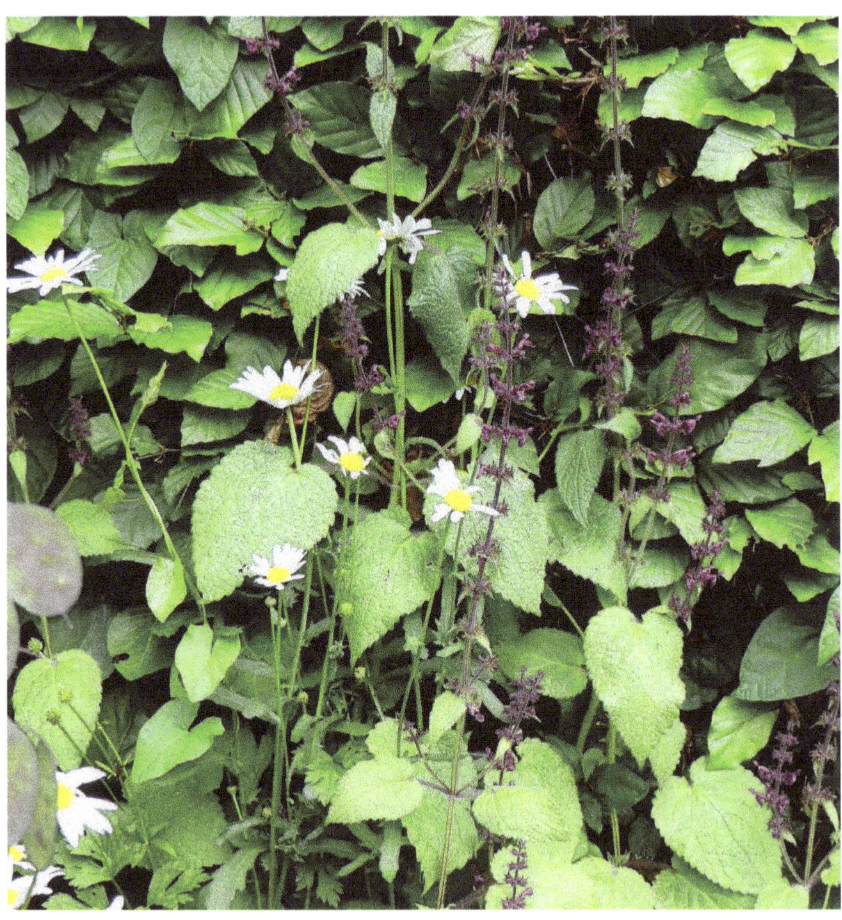

Two other wild flowers I always make sure I have are woundwort and milk thistle. I've been known to raid a neighbour's garden for both these special individuals as they are invaluable to me. Woundwort is a wound healer, tried and tested, and I'll always keep an ointment made from it in the kitchen. The leaves smell absolutely dreadful but it works for me. Herbs are my weakness – very special and very powerful little plants which are dotted all around my garden, in with the plants and wild flowers.

People think I'm mad when I tell them that herbs speak to me, and they're probably right, but touch a herb, rub its leaves between your fingers, smell its scent, and that triggers all sorts of emotions in me: holidays, childhood memories and food, to name a few.

I'm well and truly rambling now and nothing is getting done so, a freshly baked scone and tea in the garden have been consumed – simple pleasures. But even that has to come to an end as there's a cake needs jam and buttercream making. So it's back to my kitchen, cool and comforting yet warm and welcoming, to finish what I've started. I do like a job well done and a job well done is what I like to think I do.

Deer from My Doorstep, Birds from My Bed

Each and every day I pull back my bedroom curtains and gaze out across the fields before me.

Two weeks out of every four, a thirty-strong herd of red deer can be seen grazing in one of the fields beyond. The herd, a mixture of stags and hinds, will move silently across the field until they disappear into the woodland, only to appear again in late afternoon on their return journey. Why can I not ignore this regular occurrence? Why can I not just open the curtains to greet a new day and simply make my way downstairs for my first, and much-needed, cup of tea? It's impossible to do and it's why I love Exmoor so much. A new day dawns and with it comes something new to see. Yes, it's the same view but it will never look exactly the way it did yesterday, or even five minutes ago. The view from my cottage window is like a TV screen – my own personal cinema showing the latest movie.

After making my early morning cuppa I'll return to bed, and from there, while nibbling on a chocolate digestive, I am able to watch the world outside come to life. Magpies chatter noisily and land on the bare branches of the beech trees opposite, before bounding off along the tops of the hedgerows. They are busy building a nest of great proportions at the moment and are in the process of putting up the cradle part of the roof. All clever stuff!

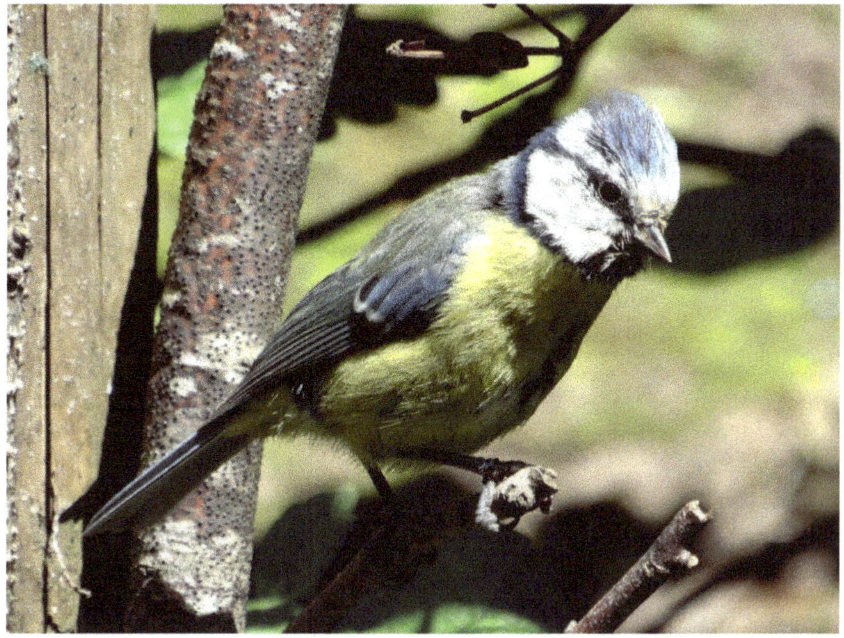

While all this is happening, very brave blue tits will come to peck at the window frames, giving me a wonderful view of their colour at this time of year. All the birds are becoming vibrant in readiness for mating but the blue tits look as if they've been to a top class salon for a makeover. They will tap on the landing window and the kitchen window but when they come to the bathroom window, they are so close you could reach out and touch them!

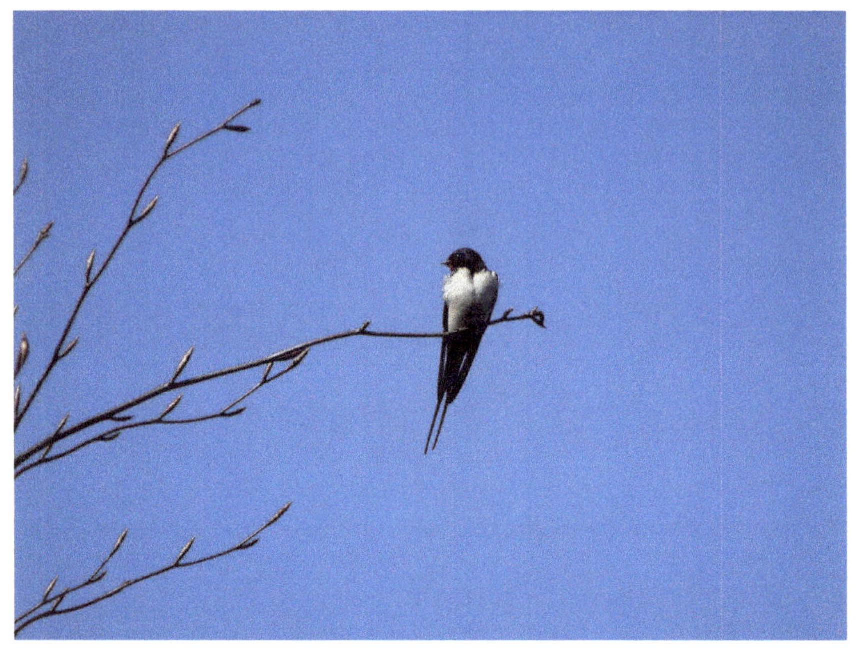

Outside the bedroom window is the cable from a telegraph pole. It snakes its way across the open sky, wobbling in the breeze to its anchor yonder, and is a stop-gap for many a bird. I'll watch for the swallows to come when the weather warms a little, their chattering constant from morning 'til night. For now though it is a regular perch for a pair of goldfinches and, together, they will sit and entertain me with their pretty faces. They will stay and use the cable for many a month to come – something to look forward to once again. Simple but priceless.

I watch the deer gradually crossing the field as I sip my tea. They split up a little and go about their business in twos and threes – the stags, still sporting their antlers, remain alone.

There is also a lone buzzard who makes an appearance some mornings – but not today. Instead I have chaffinches flitting along the hedge in abundance to keep me company, the tell-tale white bars in their tails flashing quickly as they take flight, only to land again on the floor to look for the morning's offerings. They think nothing of coming to take crumbs from the slate window sill and I'm happy to oblige.

Robins are one of my favourite birds as they are so friendly. I have three that come to visit every day and they fight like cat and dog when they happen to congregate at the bird table. They don't give off a very friendly vibe when this happens as feathers are ruffled and, more often than not, fly.

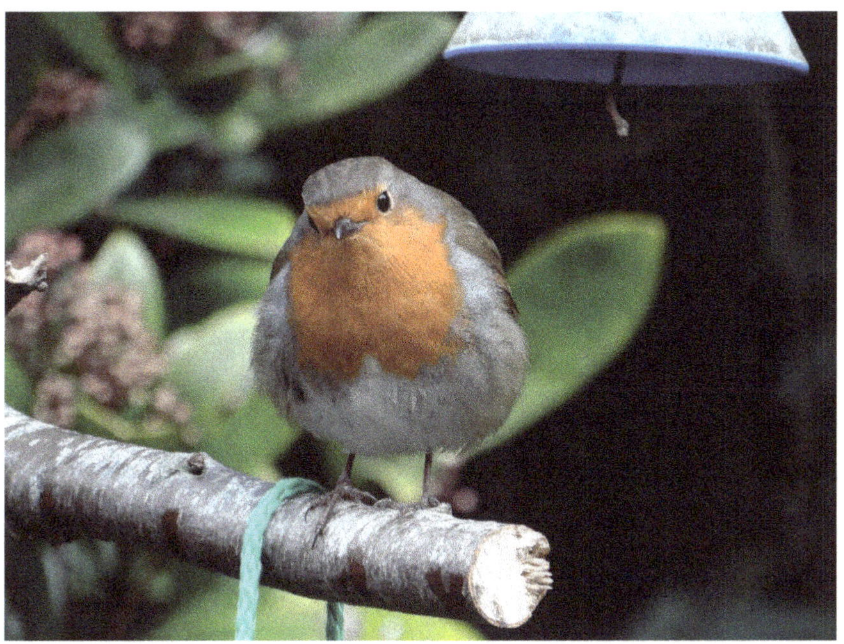

One of the robins, though, does come to sit on the old front gate and, without fail, he will be there while I dry my hair. He has a war wound to his chest and a white mark on his left wing. He'll be there this morning and if only I could drag myself away from the view, I'd probably see him there, waiting for me.

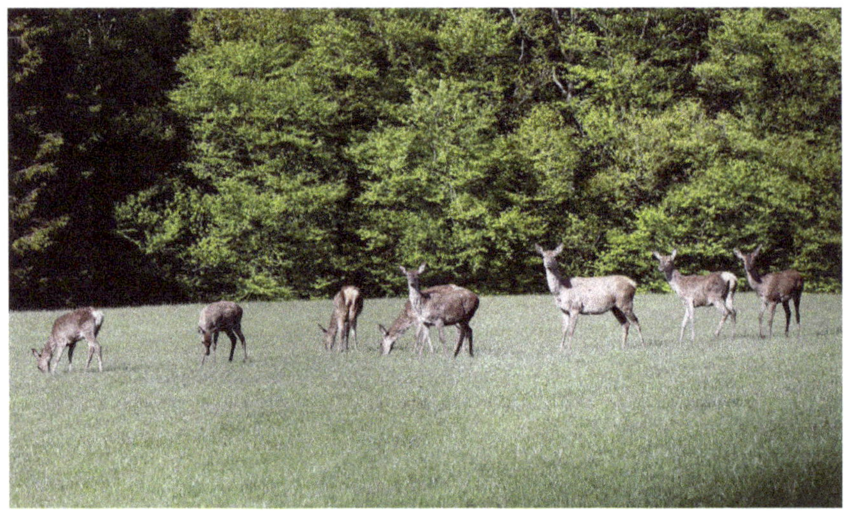

The deer, beautiful in the early morning sun, are really moving out of sight now and into the wood. It depends how the fancy takes them on where they go to next, but I can sometimes see them in the field to the right of the cottage. There they are sheltered from the lane but a little nearer to the cottage and the herd will only consist of hinds this time. Here, these wonderful creatures will settle down and make themselves comfy for a couple of hours before moving off again. It's a privilege that I'm able to see the deer on a daily basis, somewhere around the cottage. I am, by no means, a deer expert but it doesn't stop me watching them and enjoying their beauty. I am self-taught. I suppose you could say I only know what I know about them by observing. However, I read a lot, listen to others and know that I'll never stop learning.

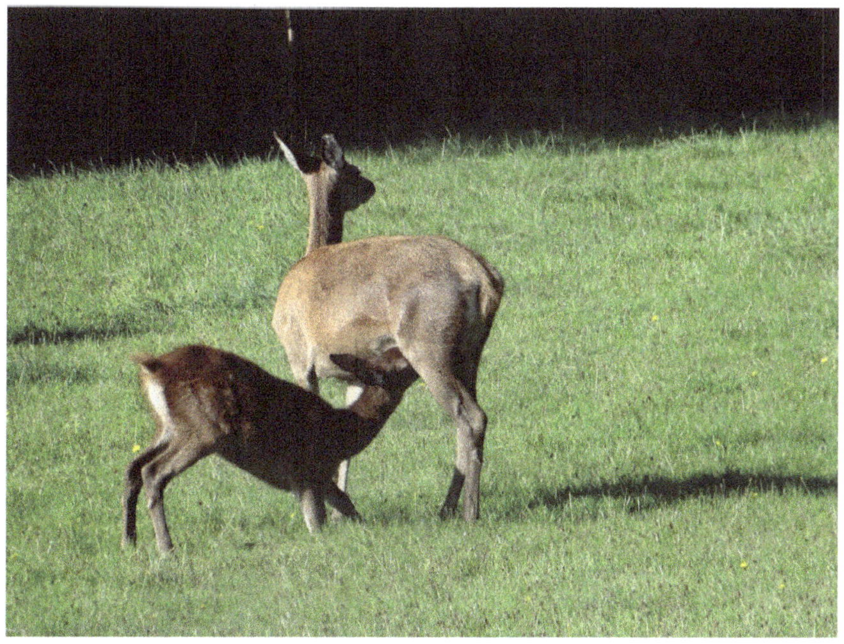

Soon enough there will be calves born to the hinds and being welcomed into the herd. Protecting these precious babies is of utmost importance, as they could be our stags of the future. Being hidden in the coarse, green bracken and long, flowing grass, they will be as safe as they can be until their mothers return. When walking the fields we have spotted many calves over the years, their two long ears blending with the habitat that they find themselves camouflaged in. It is only that we are aware that they could be about that makes us more alert in our looking as we wander. Giving these beautiful creatures a wide berth and leaving them to rest safely is paramount to their survival and growth; they are the future. In letting them rest without causing them stress, they'll be able to grow into either the kindly, balletic hind that mothered them or the grand and majestic stag that fathered them.

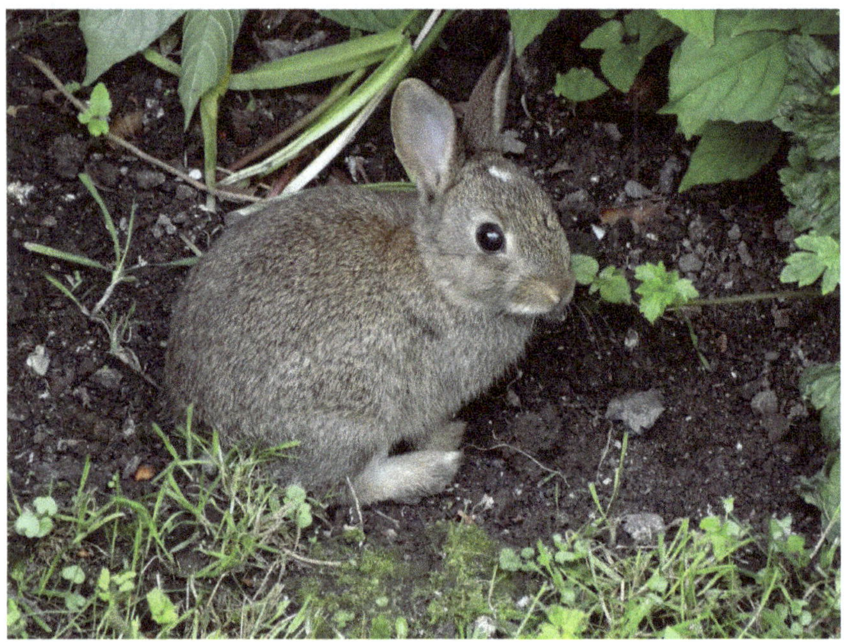

My refreshing Earl Grey finished, I now have no excuse to stay where I am. So, it's up and out and on with the day. Today's job, after the logs and sticks[1], is to investigate a large-rabbit-sized hole halfway up the garden, in the bank. I have rabbits here all the time but not exactly taking up

---

[1] My routines with logs and sticks (the latter otherwise known as 'starters and lighters') are explained in my previous books, *Exmoor Tales – Autumn* and *Exmoor Tales - Winter*

residence and I did wonder who was nibbling the tops off my dwarf daffodils. Chances are they won't be brightening my garden at Easter.

The hole is rather large, with all the earth scrabbled out and resting down the bank. It's by no means a tidy job they've made but I'll go have a look and see what needs to be done.

Baking day is normally today but the sun is shining out there and the garden needs to be investigated further than the rabbit hole. There is also a good supply of fallen sticks and branches to be had and I cannot ignore those. So, cakes and pastries may have to wait until tomorrow as herbs and seeds may keep me away, as well as 'pick up sticks', should the weather stay fine – who knows?

Whatever happens, whatever plans change, some things remain a constant in my life here: the birds and wildlife seem to cuddle this peaceful cottage of mine and the red deer of Exmoor are ever-present. These are things I will never take for granted and as I throw back my curtains each morning, greeting the world, you just might hear me proclaim, "Good morning, Exmoor. Blessed be, my friend, blessed be!"

Wandering and Weeding

Why, on a gloriously sunny Easter Monday, did I find myself on all fours removing exploding weeds from the path at the side of the cottage. Whose idea was this?

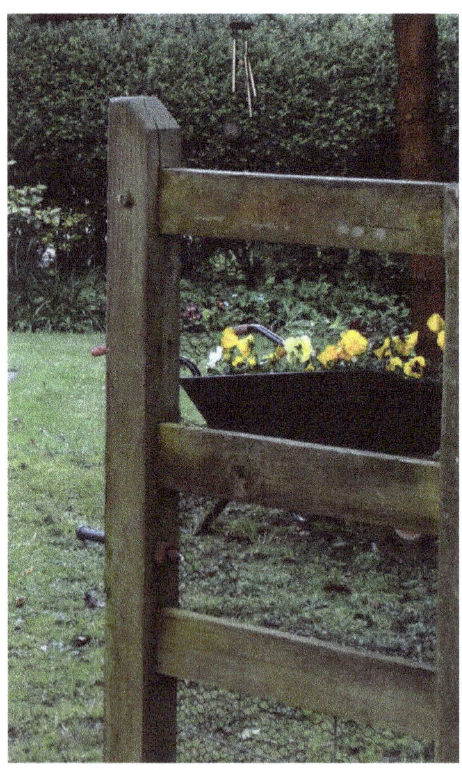

Well, it seemed like a good idea first thing this morning, before the real warmth of the sun hit my back. I had risen early and thrown back the gingham curtains only to reveal a very welcome sunny morning and a forty-strong gathering of red deer in the field beyond. The morning sun turned their coats to a stunning orangey-ginger colour, and they shone like new copper-coloured pennies. A couple of the stags still had their antlers, but not for much longer, I thought.

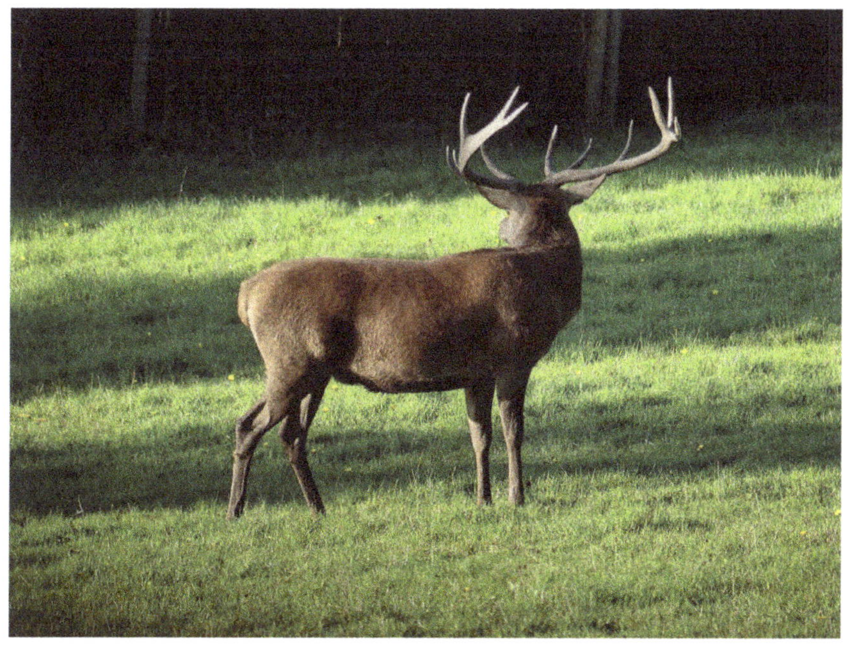

So I was up, chores completed, bird table replenished, and feeders filled, and still had the whole day in front of me. I sat with yet another cup of tea and a toasted cherry hot cross bun at the kitchen window, pondering my day. I normally try to have a 'job of the day' so that I can fit everything in, but when the weather turns up trumps plans have to be altered, for there are so many good-weather jobs to be done – weeding being one of them.

So, there I was, on my hands and knees, pulling out my unwanted intruders. But as the sun grew warmer I felt the need to remove a layer of clothing and thought that today

I'd let the weeds feel free to explode. Free! Just like me – because I was taking myself off for a wander.

My nearest neighbours are half a mile away in each direction, and here at the cottage I am surrounded by their land, made up of woodland and fields that dip into stunningly beautiful coombes and valleys. I find myself very privileged to have the run of this land, free to wander at my leisure, to enjoy the pathways and wildlife thereon.

Across the way, down the lane, is a solid five-bar gate and it is over the gate that I headed. I had supplies with me: chocolate, mints, and an apple. Enough to keep me going, as I was only out for a wander.

My walk took me over two pasture fields to start with, inhabited by ewes and their new lambs. The lambs were so new that a few were still wrinkly around the legs and hadn't completely found their feet yet. The older ones seemed to enjoy a game of jumping up onto mum's back while she was trying to have a nap, or cavorting and gambolling about with their mates. At this time of year, I enjoy hearing the ewes and lambs calling to each other throughout the day and into the night. Sounds of the countryside – another simple pleasure.

I have a habit of stopping to lean on gates, to take in the scene before me, because so much is missed if you don't stop awhile and look. I look, up, over, around, and always down.

I had not walked very far before I clocked that the warmth of the sun over the last days had encouraged the primroses to adorn the ancient Exmoor banks and hedgerows. These pretty flowers, in the most delicate shade of lemon, were in clumps everywhere! Keeping them company, and not really bothering where they grew, were brightly coloured yellow celandine – not as much in abundance but still making their presence felt. The snowdrops, in the green, were gone for another year.

Perched on a leafless beech tree was a kestrel, who is always around this particular spot. I watched him for a while as he flew from tree to fence post and back again. He always uses the fields and various resting points to his advantage.

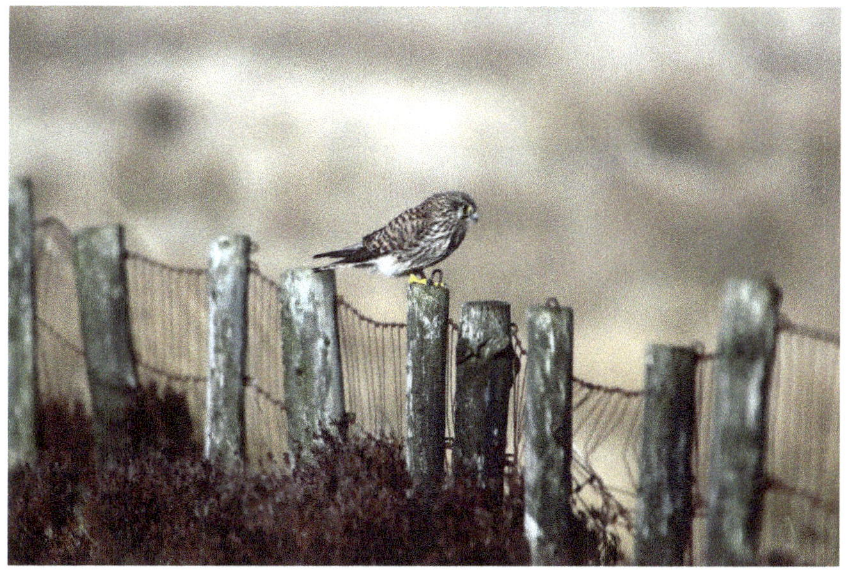

Over the valley and looking towards moorland, I spotted a small herd of deer. They were all hinds and were resting in a corner of a sloping field, enjoying the sun and at peace. One remained standing, grazing, but keeping an ear open for any danger, I guess. My path took me down a steep field and I kept to the edge, as I always do, out of respect to the farmers who allow me to walk their land.

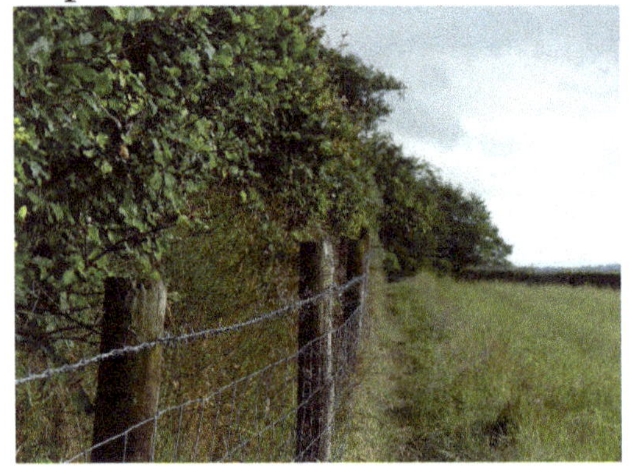

Over a stile at the end and I was in sparse woodland, where the deer have carved out pathways along the fence and through the trees. The path was dotted with muddy puddles and shaded from the sun but I ploughed on through as quietly as I could, looking about me as I went.

Coming out into another field at the bottom of the slope I passed a large rabbit warren. It was in use, as there were droppings nearby and the earth was freshly dug around the main entrance, which was huge.

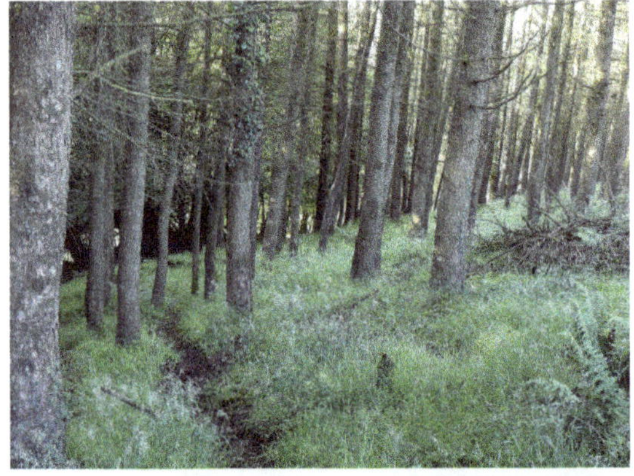

In the summer most of this area is covered in lush, green ferns and you'd be hard pressed to locate the rabbits' hideaway if you

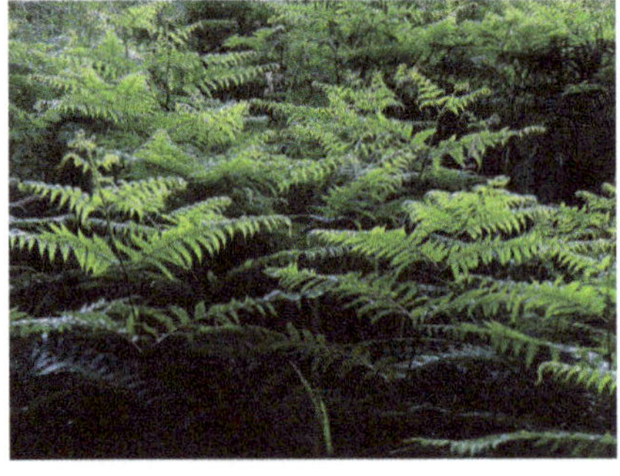

didn't know where it was to[2]. Badgers roam this field too. Their sett is not far from the rabbit residence but is safely tucked away in the wood, on the other side of the fence. Their trails were clearly marked by the flattened grass and earth, and I stopped there for a while to eat my apple and chocolate. There was another gate to lean on, so why not?

Usually, down there, I'd be able to watch the buzzards as they called to one another. They're here every year and use two old beech trees as cover. They are able to soar high above this beautiful valley and spacious woodland but also have the benefit of open grassland too. Snack finished and I was on my way again.

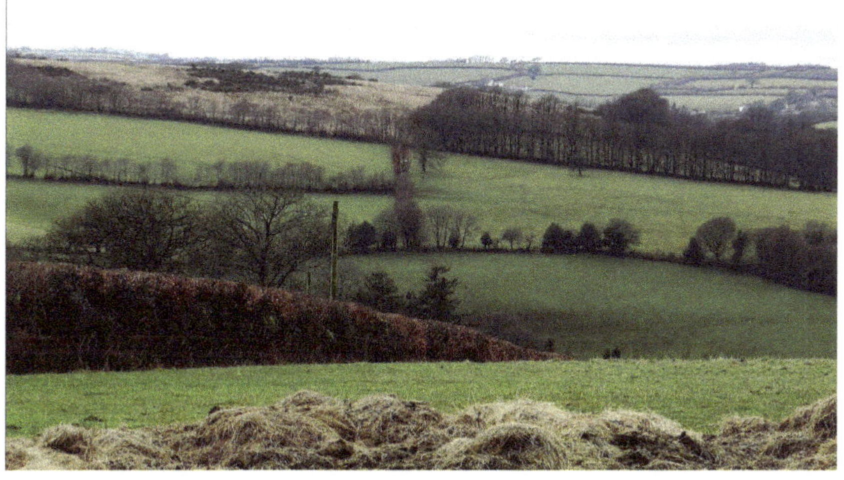

Climbing the gate, I found myself back in the woodland. It was easy to walk quietly there, on the carpet of soggy

---

[2] This use of 'to' is Devon dialect. You'll often hear someone enquiring after a friend's whereabouts with 'where's he to?'

leaves and pine needles. I stood and looked about me as I took a pathway that skirted a grassy field protected by beech hedges and trees. After a few minutes of walking I spied, in the field to my right, several red deer. They had been sitting down but two were now on their feet, noses in the air. They didn't bark their warning sound though; no matter how many times I hear that, it scares the pants off me for it is so loud! Out here in the woodland it's even worse, for if the deer see you before you see them, their bark is quite unexpected and I have been known to leave the floor at the sound of it.

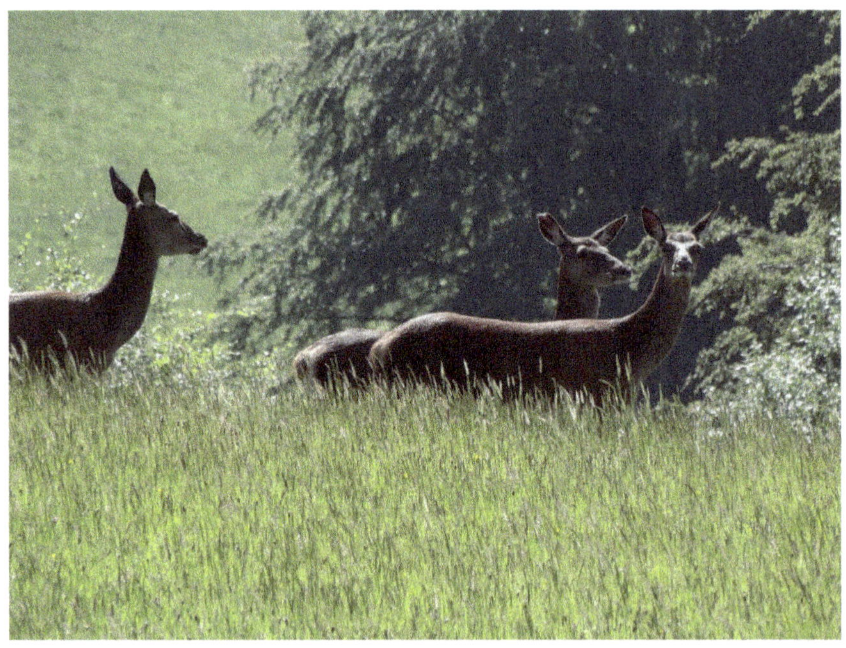

I really didn't want to disturb them but wanted to watch them awhile, so I crouched down behind a tree and tried not to move. They were fully aware of my presence as the two remained standing, keeping watch, but they were relaxed enough to put their heads down and graze. I peeped out from my hiding place and watched those beautiful creatures for a while, taking in the sunshine, secluded and safe. To me, that was Exmoor at its finest; I know I'm so lucky to be able to witness such an idyllic scene.

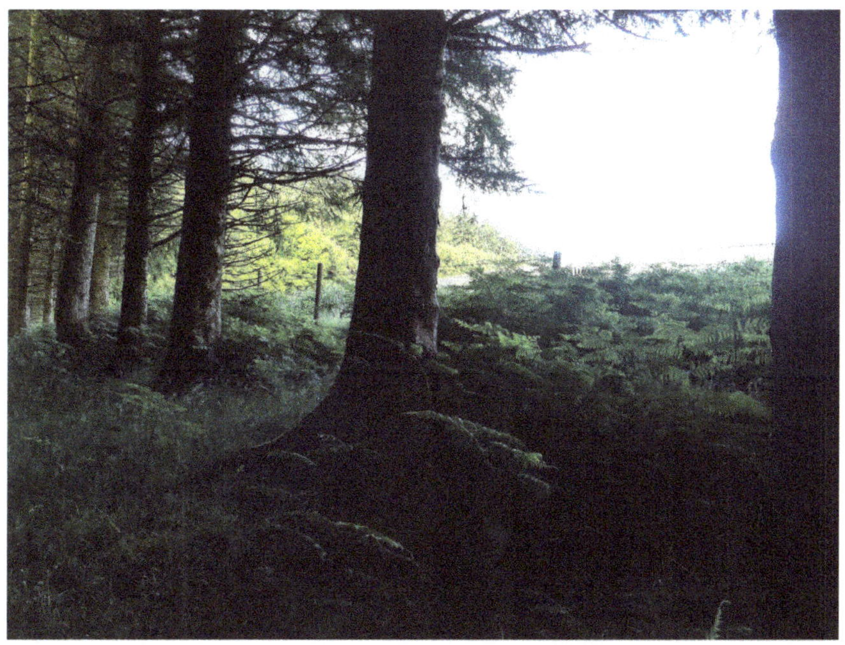

Off once again, and leaving the deer behind me, I walked on. I could hear the river from there but couldn't see it. However, I was not going in that direction but instead quietly picked my way over lush, damp, mossy humps, listening to birdsong as I went. I was homeward bound, on a circular route that would take me via the woods.

The soggy path was caked with muddy puddles and I made my way uphill, past the wallow where the deer come to bathe in the mud. The sun doesn't shine down through the canopy of trees so much and the wallow keeps wet and damp for many months of the year. It's well used, and the deer slots are of differing sizes around it. I was in a part of the woods where the deer are always seen. They will come into the fields at any time of day, leaping over the fence from a standing position with immense grace. A couple more gates to go and the cottage would be in sight.

More pasture land took me home. Two more fields, flanked on one side by blackberries, the stems of which will reach out and cover the hedgerows throughout summer. Juicy fruits 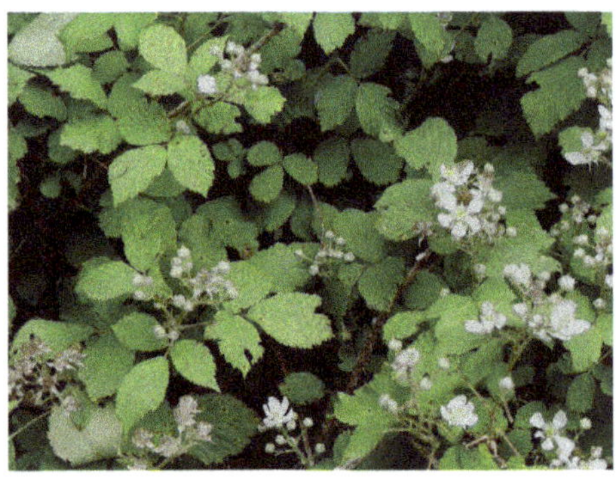 harvested in September will make pies, crumbles, and jams to be stored for treats during the winter months. What glories to look forward to!

My wander took two hours out of the morning, but what better way to spend time than out in the open, sharing the delights of our countryside? So, the weeding stills awaits me but it can wait ten minutes more, surely, while I make myself a chai latte and sit on my bench, contemplating just how much exploding the weeds have done in my absence.

Early Evening on the Moor

After a beautifully warm and sunny day there seemed no other way to end it than by taking a drive up and over the moor in the early evening, as the sun was preparing to say goodnight. So that's what I am doing. I love trips out at this time of day. It's a chance to see the moor in a different light and there's a chance you'll see far more than you bargained for. Coat, camera, and binoculars in the car, a body warmer and gloves at the ready (it can become pretty chilly, quite quickly), a steaming hot coffee safely in the cup holder, and I'm set to go.

I have no idea what I'll see but I've walked out on the washing up, so it had better be something good! A short-eared owl has been attracting photographers and enthusiasts alike, so I know where I'm headed. I was lucky enough to see one this time last year, in the same spot, and would love to see it again, before it sets off to its nesting destination. It feels good to be out and about, doing what I love, and it doesn't bother me in the slightest that I have congealed dinner plates awaiting me on my return.

The Exmoor ponies have foals at the moment and some are older than others. However, to the right of me, on the roadside, there is the smallest specimen I have ever seen – it takes my breath away!

With the car stopped, I watch as this tiny, ginger-coated foal goes to suckle, its patient mother standing while the foal has its fill. The other ponies bunch around the mother and look for all the world as if they are her circle of protection, while she feeds her baby. Once the baby is content, they all wander off in a group together, across the moor and into the last of the evening sun.

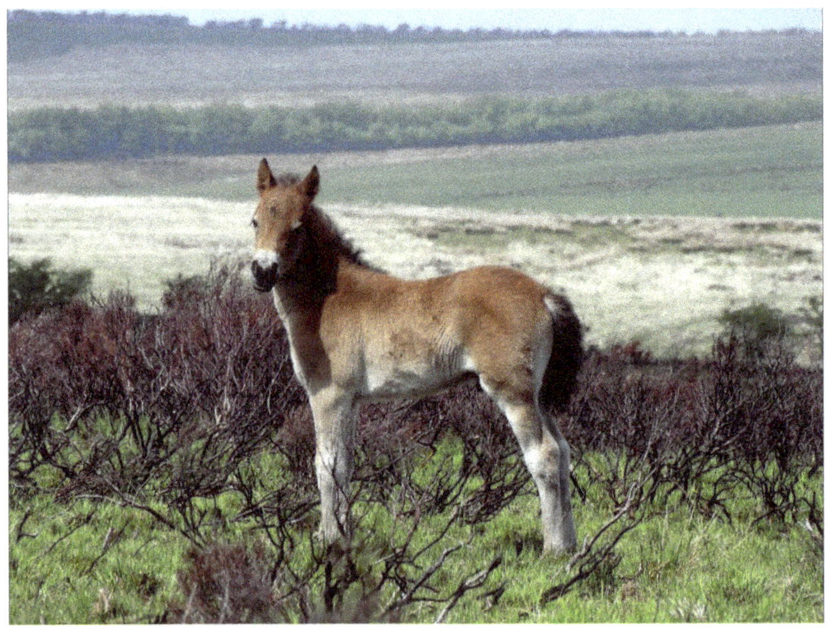

Yellow gorse bushes line the road here and you have to be on your guard constantly. Not only do ponies graze and wander hereabouts but cattle, sheep, and deer do too. Any one of these animals could appear from where road meets moor, so you must have your eyes peeled and your wits about you. 'Expect the unexpected' is always a good motto. Even more so at this time of the evening.

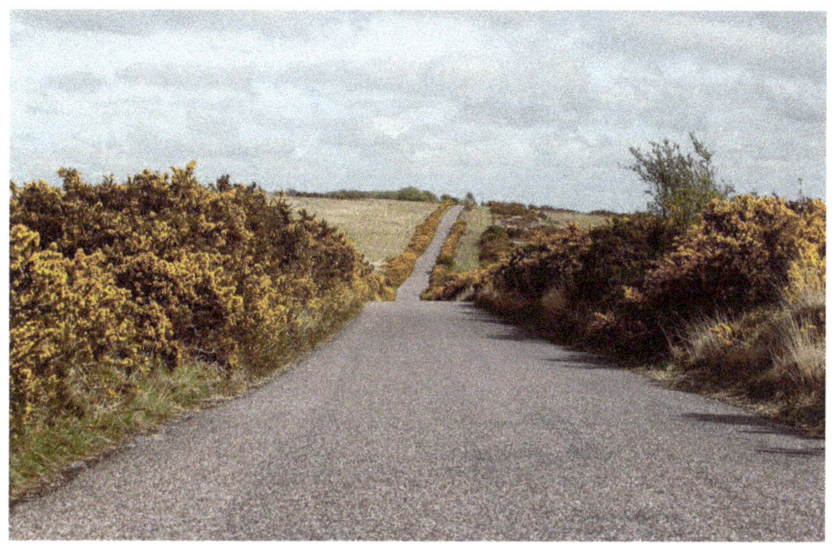

I love the colours that the moor throws up at different times of the day. Everything seems to have a glow about it while the sun is doing its thing in settling down for the night – and the sky is no exception.

As I near my destination, the sky before me is turning a lilac blue with tinges of burnt ochre on the horizon. Standing atop a ridge there are three red deer stags (and maybe a fourth, minus its antlers). They are silhouetted against the evening sky and it's moments like this that make my heart sing. They appear majestic in their stance, proud to be what they are, even though they are probably near to losing their most precious asset: their antlers. But it doesn't prevent them from standing for a while, proving they're a cracking good subject for the camera!

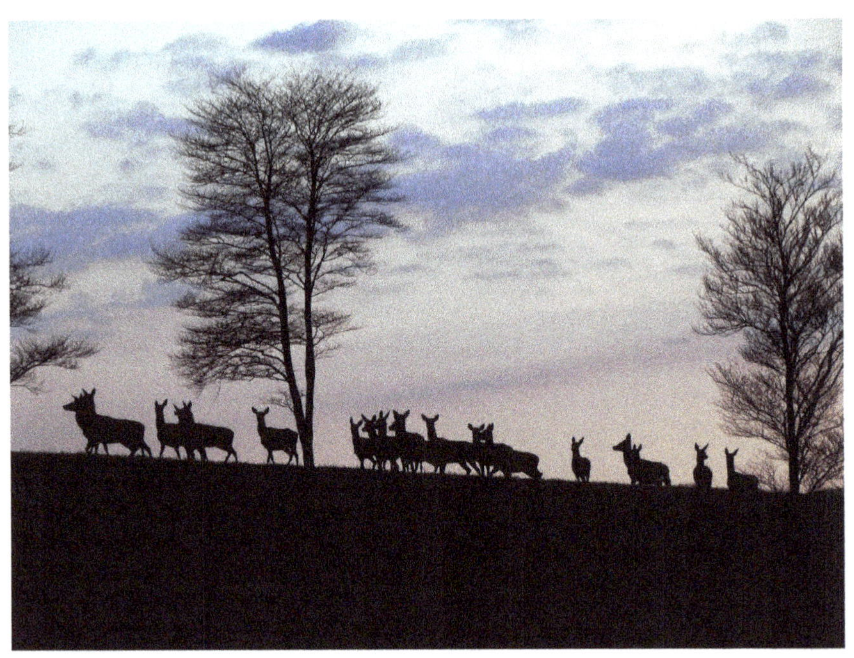

I'm parked up at the end of a lane. The mood is quiet; there is a peacefulness up here that stills the heart and calms the soul. A pair of buzzards glide about the sky against the setting sun, and several crows swoop from post to post, their blackness eerie against the early evening backdrop, their cawing loud in the stillness.

From out of the corner of my eye, I catch a movement on the common land to the left of me. Black ear tips are a treasure that I'm always on the lookout for, because they show me that a hare is in view … and there it is! My most favourite of all animals. A hare of great proportions, facing away from me and ready for the off. But that doesn't matter, I've caught sight of it. Whether it's off like a shot from a gun, or stays awhile for me to take a photo, is neither here nor there – it's yet another memory to put in the box.

As it happens, it was off, bounding away across the earth, zigzagging as it made its way to cover at the side of the field, where it went from sight. That angular, sometimes gaunt-looking face, the ranging gait, and those ears – absolutely amazing. I love them!

So, I'm off to see if I can find the short-eared owl, which holds an amber status and is well worth a sighting. It's mottled brown in colour, has a pretty face and is full of character.

As I walk towards a junction in the lane, looking for a good waiting post, said owl comes flying towards me, flying low over the grassy moorland. I hadn't expected it and, although my camera is at the ready, I miss my moment as I'm too busy looking and am caught off guard. Fine photographer I am! But it's lithe in its movement, silent and very, very beautiful. The owl flies right at me. I am stood in the corner, behind a bush and because of the bush I lose sight of it. The owl comes to a halt on a post, resting and out of my view, just the other side of the hedge. The situation is totally frustrating but that's wildlife for you. However, I have seen it and am happy to take that home with me.

I wait for another hour or so, with some very good company (out with the same aim as me) before deciding it is getting chilly. In the meantime, I am fully entertained by a herd of red deer, about fifty of them, over the moor, grazing in a field. They bunch together, spread out, bunch up again, moving as they feed. It doesn't matter where you are on Exmoor, there will always be something to delight you. It may not be what you set out to see, but go with an open mind and you'll never be disappointed.

Back in the warmth of the car, I pop a liquorice allsort in my mouth (one of those jelly ones covered with bobbly bits – not my favourite at all but it will suffice until I arrive home).

My camera is out and at the ready. As the evening is turning into dusk now, I know my camera will struggle with the lack of light very soon but I'll take my chances. As I move slowly back along the lane, I spot a kestrel flying up from a grassy field. At first glance, and side on, I thought it was the owl, but no.

Onwards then I go, homeward bound to my cottage and the promise of a hot cup of Earl Grey and a slice of homemade Victoria sponge in front of the TV, before bed and a good book.

The sun has just disappeared in a blaze of glory; the sky is calming down from its fiery appearance to gentler, softer tones now the sun has gone from us. I've witnessed yet another Exmoor sunset and I know that I'll never tire of them. A couple more photos are taken for the album. It's hard to resist such beauty.

A chance look to the left of me and there the short-eared owl sits, on a round fence post. I thought it had gone for the evening but, no, it had hung around to wish me goodnight. Distance wasn't a problem for my camera but the fading light was. I managed some shots but they're not up to much. Never mind, I'd seen it; it was there in all its glory and I'll take that as a successful evening.

Return journey, here I come and, as I travel the lanes home, a myriad of creatures keep me company. First is the rural fox, out for the evening on the hunt for his dinner. Large, rusty-coloured, and with a superb brush and white tip, he trots gently along the 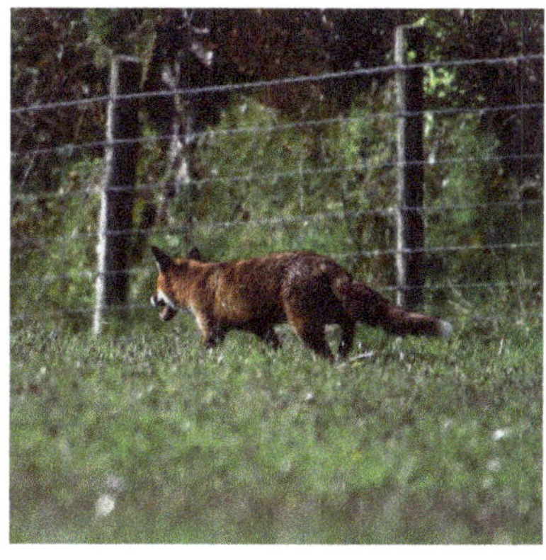 lane in front of me, nose down on the ground. He finds a gap in the beech hedge, where he can move out of the way. Next, a buzzard, swooping low up and over a hedge, a dark outline in the now twilight sky, off to who knows where. Then the red deer, out on the great expanse of moorland where they are happily grazing. In this light it's hard to distinguish between gorse bushes and deer, if they have their heads down, although that might just be me. But their heads are up, they're dark against the skyline and number around fifteen. I slow to watch them but am loathe to spook them, so drive on towards my cottage.

Home is in sight now; the outside light guides me in. I stand in the semi-darkness beside the beech hedge, the lambs are bleating and the tawny owls are calling out to each other across the lane. I'll be able to lie and listen to them as I fall asleep. What a perfect end to a perfect day.

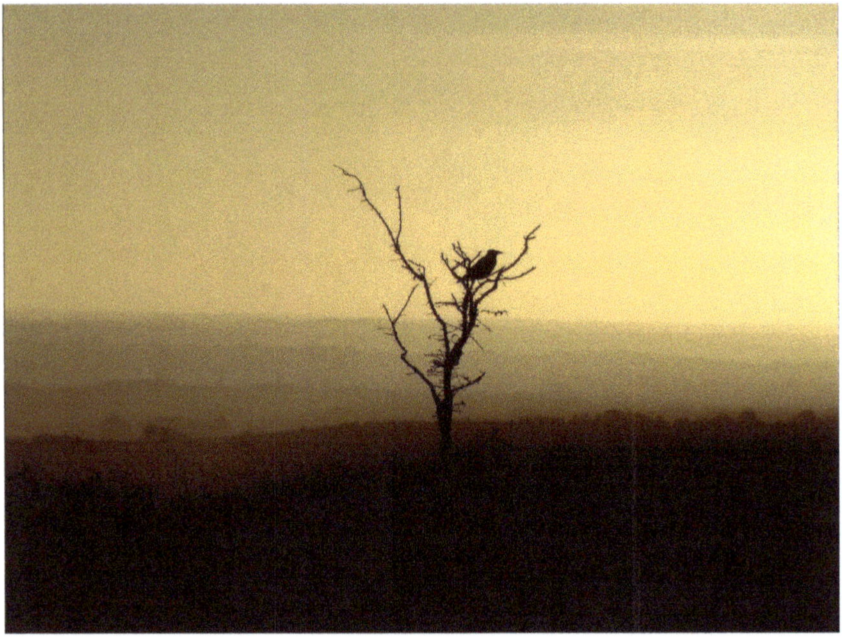

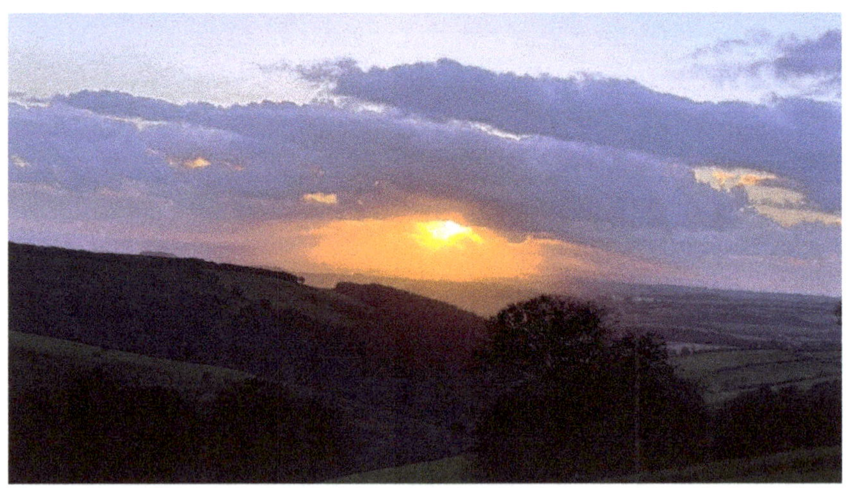

About the Author

Ellie is the wrong side of sixty (her own words). She is married with two grown-up children, loves to be outdoors, and now lives on Exmoor with her husband. Originally moving to Somerset in 2004, she began writing thoughts about her life on the moor around 2013, a year before her youngest grandson was born. She felt that she needed to start a diary of sorts: in this way all three of her grandchildren would be able to learn what her life was like on Exmoor. Not having that kind of information about her own parents or grandparents, it spurred her on to making a record for them, so that they, too, would fall in love with the place where she lived. Writing from her Exmoor cottage, a cup of lemon-and-ginger tea to hand, together with a slice of homemade cake, Ellie knows that she has come home.

Acknowledgements

My husband accompanies me when we are out and about or simply working in the garden. He's less available when I'm cooking, although he does appear when it's tasting time. It is mostly thanks to him that we have some wonderful photos to bring my words to life; he is a diamond and also the glue that holds me together when my confidence fails me.

I must thank the custodians of the cottage whence I've penned my stories. They know who they are. The cottage is the heartbeat of my words and without its presence, and their understanding, I may not have started writing at all.

I cannot go forward without mentioning the inimitable Johnny Kingdom. He was an inspiration to my husband and me as well as a good friend. The kindness he showed, and knowledge he imparted, is everlasting.

My final thanks go to Olli at Blue Poppy Publishing. Thank you for seeing something in my words that others couldn't or wouldn't. You have made me smile, jump up and down, and cry, all at the same time, and I cannot thank you enough for giving me the chance to have a book published for my three amazing grandchildren; your help has been priceless. Sink or swim, it will be a legacy left for them, for always.

About Blue Poppy Publishing

Blue Poppy Publishing is a small independent publisher with big ambitions. It started in Ilfracombe in 2016 when Oliver Tooley wanted to give his self-published novel an air of credibility. The name was inspired by Oliver's grandfather, Frank Kingdon-Ward, who famously collected the first viable seed of *Meconopsis betonicifolia*, the Himalayan blue poppy. Blue Poppy Publishing now has dozens of titles by twenty or more authors but still has a way to go to compete with the big guns.

As a small business we depend on word-of-mouth far more than others so please, if you have enjoyed this book, tell others, write a review, blog about it, post on social media.

This book is the third in a four-part series, with one title for each season. *Autumn* and *Winter* are already available online or from all good UK bookshops, *Spring* will hit shops in March 2023 and then *Summer* will be available in May.

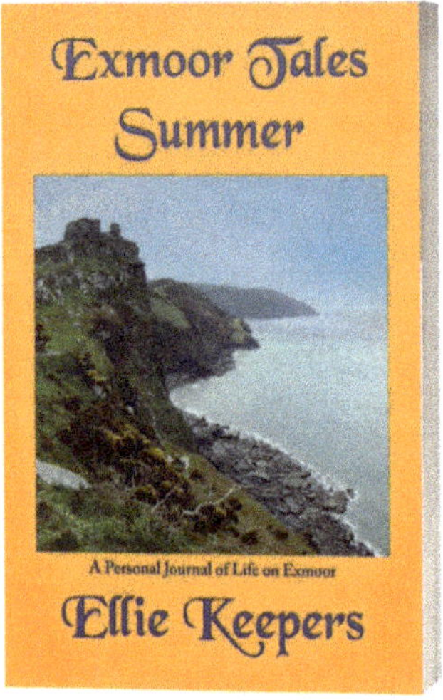

If you enjoyed reading about Exmoor in spring then why not add the remaining three books in the series.

Each volume includes many more stories of life on Exmoor, accompanied by more of Ellie's stunning full-colour photography.

Summer ISBN: 978-1-83778-004-4

Autumn ISBN: 978-1-83778-001-3

Winter　ISBN: 978-1-83778-002-0

Order Autumn and Winter from bookshops worldwide, or direct from www.bluepoppypublishing.co.uk

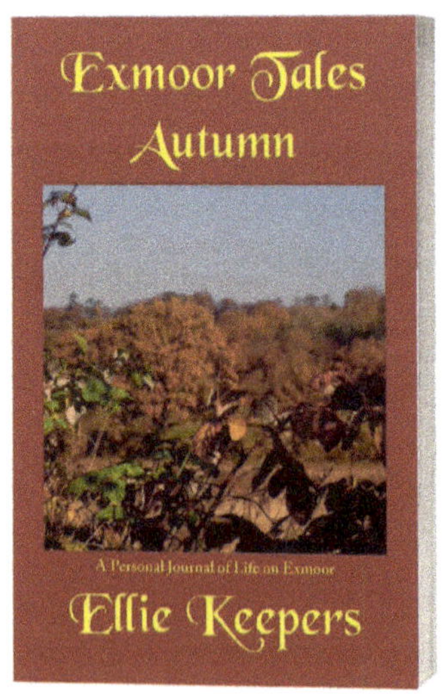

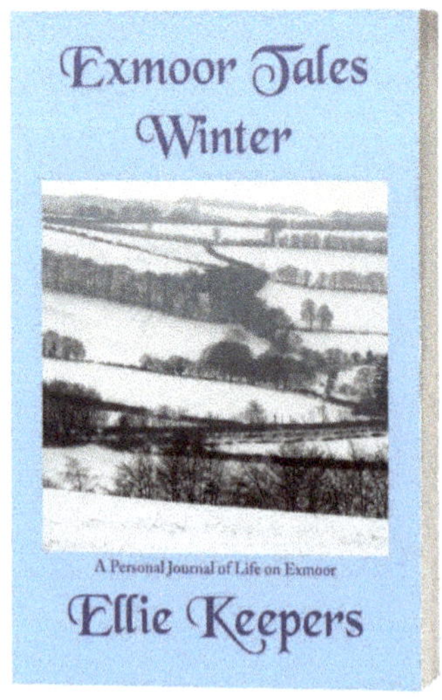